SHORT CUTS IN FAMILY HISTORY

An Introduction to Planning Research

MICHAEL GANDY

COUNTRYSIDE BOOKS
NEWBURY, BERKSHIRE

First Published by FFHS 1993
2nd edition 1994
Revised and updated 1998

COUNTRYSIDE BOOKS
3 Catherine Road
Newbury, Berkshire
and
THE FEDERATION OF
FAMILY HISTORY SOCIETIES
The Benson Room, Birmingham & Midland Institute,
Margaret Street, Birmingham B3 3BS

ISBN 1 85306 316 9

Designed by Mon Mohan

Produced through MRM Associates Ltd., Reading
Typeset by Paragon Typesetters, Clwyd
Printed by Woolnough Bookbinding, Irthlingborough

CONTENTS

FOREWORD

The majority of records relating to English ancestors will be found either in the record office of the county where they lived or in the great national collections which are in London. Thus almost everyone finds that research is slowed down or made more expensive by the fact that most of us no longer live in the same place as our ancestors. This booklet is intended to help you get most use out of occasional visits to distant repositories by careful planning and doing your preparatory homework as thoroughly as possible.

It is assumed that the reader has a knowledge of the basic sources and procedures in genealogy; in the following pages I run through the main stages of research, adding what I hope are useful tips and warnings.

In the course of the text I refer to various booklets, indexes and services. Details of these are given in Appendix I which lists publications by the Federation of Family History Societies, Society of Genealogists, Public Record Office, Institute of Heraldic and Genealogical Studies and others. If you use these prime sources properly you will have no difficulty getting current information about many others.

Michael Gandy
1998

ABBREVIATIONS USED IN THE TEXT

C of E	Church of England, also called the Anglican Church
FRC	Family Records Centre
GRO	General Register Office
IHGS	Institute of Heraldic and Genealogical Studies
CRO	County Record Office
PRO	Public Record Office
FHS	Family History Society
FFHS	Federation of Family History Societies
SoG	Society of Genealogists
BTs	Bishops' Transcripts (copies of the parish registers sent in annually to the Bishop)
IGI	International Genealogical Index
LDS	Church of Jesus Christ of Latter Day Saints, also called Mormons
LMA	London Metropolitan Archives, formerly known as the Greater London Record Office (GLRO)

SOME GENERAL POINTS

Family history is among the most popular hobbies in the UK today and hundreds of thousands of people have discovered the pleasure of compiling an accurate and provable family tree and of reading up on the life-styles and occupations of their ancestors anywhere in the country over the last five or six centuries. However, many beginners spend a good deal of unnecessary time because they have not keyed in to a whole series of short cuts which can take some of the hard work out of the search – or just speed things up – without taking away any of the pleasure.

Time versus money

In tracing your family history – just as in gardening, home decoration, car maintenance – there is a basic choice between spending your time or spending your money.

If you live near the right repository and have plenty of free time you can, for example, read through dozens of wills to see which relate to your family and this may not cost you a penny. If you live a long way away and have to allow for fares, meals, accommodation or even lost working time then it may be both cheaper and quicker to order photocopies by post to read at leisure at home. Ten or twenty pounds on photocopies may be worthwhile even if the records turn out to be irrelevant, and if they turn out to be relevant you would have wanted photocopies anyway. Even if you are at the record office, ordering photocopies to work on later will leave you free to spend the time on other material with the added bonus that if there is anything you can't read or don't understand you can keep showing it to your friends (ex-friends if you do it too often!) until you find someone who can explain it to you.

When you know exactly what needs to be done but haven't the time to do it, or if you are not confident with Latin and old handwriting, then it may be quicker and more efficient to use a professional record searcher. A list of these is published by the Association of Genealogists and Record Agents (the SoG and your local FHS bookstall have this): other lists may be available through CROs. The PRO and the India Office Library have names and many more advertise in *Family Tree Magazine* and *Practical Family Tree* (which are easily available through W H Smith or any newsagent) and the *Genealogists' Magazine* (the journal of the Society of Genealogists).

Most researchers who advertise are only semi-professional in the sense that they do not earn their main living from the work and this is good from the client's point of view because it means they are cheap. Many of them got their expertise through doing an increasing amount for friends or FHS members and they are mostly on our wavelength. Often they have specialised in some category of records which related to their own ancestry or just took their fancy and are therefore the world expert on that little area. On the negative side, many semi-professionals don't know much more than you do. Tell them what to do or discuss it with them and you will probably get a good job done; leave it to them and you may find that they haven't got any better ideas than you could have had yourself. Let them be your arms, legs and eyes but use your own brain. For specialist, professional knowledge, naturally, you must expect to pay more (recommended minimum rate £15 an hour).

There are now an enormous number of cheap lists, indexes, catalogues, maps, directories, microfiche and microfilm transcripts that you can borrow or buy to use at home. It gets steadily easier to find out what sources exist, what survives, where it is, when and how it can be seen. Many people waste time because they have not realised that this parish has not deposited its registers, that parish has none because they were destroyed, these records are away being microfilmed or those records have to be fetched in from an out-repository which

Old handwriting is not easy to decipher without practice, as this will of John Chalkeley of Bendish, Herts dated 1557 shows. You may want to consider employing a professional researcher for some tasks – time versus money, it's your choice! (1AW24, courtesy Herts Record Office)

needs three days notice. In some cases, original material is available in one place while an indexed transcript is available elsewhere.

Some repositories have a good deal of material on open access or can fetch most things quickly from storerooms nearby; others have rules about how many documents you can have at one time or will only fetch material at certain times. If combined with an unhelpful catalogue, this sort of thing can mean your day drifts by in waiting rather than researching. One CRO, for example, used to have its Bishops' Transcripts arranged by deanery in five year periods – perfect if you wanted to do a blanket search of an area but irritating if you wanted to search 50 years of a tiny parish. One very large record office used to have every year of its BTs in every parish catalogued as a separate piece and would only produce three at a time. BTs were definitely not a short cut in that record office!

Basic research guides are the indispensable tools of our trade and you should find these, as well as a range of local history publications, on the bookstall at your local FHS meeting; otherwise write to the SoG and FFHS for their book lists. If the specific information you want is not available in these books then a phone call or letter to the relevant repository may save a wasted visit.

You should always contact a repository in advance to say you want to visit, especially in the holiday seasons when many offices get booked up well in advance and if you turn up without an appointment they may have to send you away. Even if you can get in, you may not be able to use a microfilm and microfiche reader or the special table for large maps. The addresses and telephone numbers of all the usual repositories are detailed in *Record Offices: How To Find Them* (a Gibson Guide published by the FFHS) which gives a map for each area and shows the bus and railway station and local car parks.

SUMMARY: Time versus money – you decide. Consider using a professional – for expert work; for work at a distance; if you're too busy and don't want to wait. Prepare thoroughly before visiting an archive.

Working with a friend

Naturally it is nice to travel with a friend or interested relative but when you get to the repository, part company and do your research on your own. If you are both working on the same families then sort out a division of labour before you start and leave each other alone.

Flora Thompson in *Lark Rise to Candleford* (a social history must) quotes the old Oxfordshire saying: 'One boy's a boy, two boys are half a boy and three boys are no boy at all'. If you keep chatting to your friend you won't concentrate, you'll start arguing about what you know already (We never argue, we just discuss!) and what you ought to do about what you've just found, you'll have to break for lunch or coffee whenever your friend wants to and altogether you won't get as much done as you would on your own. Sometimes it works if one of you is in charge and the other is a willing slave but even then your endless chit-chat and instructions will put everybody else off. You may not need silence if you're only giving half your mind to a simple parish register; your neighbour does need silence while he wrestles with Latin, handwriting and dirt in a manor court roll or tries to take in how chancery court records are arranged. Anyway, while you chat you'll miss the entry you're looking for and that's not a short cut to anything!

Did you notice I said an *interested* relative? Never take your husband, mother or children with you unless they really want to come. Above all, if you have young children do not involve them. Let us leave aside that your children are a damned pest to everyone else (mine, of course, are charming). They will lose interest very quickly, they will sprawl on the floor and whine, they will keep saying 'When are we going, Mummy?' and eventually you will lose patience and concentration and if you take them to the park afterwards you will already have spoilt the day. 'What do you remember about your ancestors, Uncle Jim?' 'We had a nasty time whenever my mother was looking for them.' If you have young children and no one to leave them with then forget about record offices for a few years. Almost anyone whose children are grown up will tell you to enjoy those few years while they are still little – no hobby is worth it if it makes you nag your kids.

Not that family history can't be fun for children if you let them approach it in their way. However, they don't necessarily want to spend all their holidays on it. Once when we were out driving, our daughter Rachel (then about ten) pointed out of the window and said, 'Oh, look at that!' General turning of heads but we couldn't see anything particular. 'What are we

looking at?' 'Oh, nothing, but there was a graveyard on the other side and I thought you might want to get out.'
SUMMARY: Go with a friend but don't work with a friend. Don't go with anyone who doesn't really *want* to go.

Seeing your ancestors' world through their eyes

This is practically impossible of course but we have to try. Some people (eg historical novelists and television producers) seem to think of our ancestors as exactly like ourselves but wearing different clothes, while others think of them as so different from us that we can ascribe almost any opinion to them, however much our common sense revolts. The truth is not only in between but depends upon what century, county, age, temperament, sex or class we are talking about. Generalisations about our ancestors are just as valid as generalisations about us; that is, not very.

However, that said, we can find out a great deal about the facts of their lives: their work, travel, housing, diet, religion (but what their denomination believed then – not what it believes now). Depending on these social factors, our ancestors would be more likely to do or be one thing than another. Our ancestors were not like an American family in a sit-com ('Gee, dad, can we talk?' 'Sure, son. Come into the den.') but they were not brutal, superstitious peasants either.

A sailor would marry 50 miles along the coast rather than five miles inland. A 17th century ancestor who was a lawyer could never have been a Baptist and vice versa. Poor Irish ancestors in Liverpool might be Protestant or Catholic but in London they were almost certain to be Catholic. Very few Cheshire people would move to Wiltshire – unless they were railwaymen going from Crewe to Swindon. Although the majority of Huguenots were in London, the West End ones and the East End ones wouldn't mix much because they were of different classes. People often mention Victorian morality and talk as if our 19th century ancestors lived shocked, narrow and rigid lives but they had far more babies than we do and lived much closer to animals even in the towns, while their rate of first-child

Trying to see our ancestors' world through their eyes, such as this young man of the 1880s, is part of the fun of family history, but we have to be careful not to impose our own ideas and prejudices on the past.

conception outside marriage was far higher than ours. On the other hand, teenage marriage, which became reasonably (but not very) frequent in the poorer parts of industrial towns, was quite out of the question for men and women in the 17th and 18th century countryside. If your tree links a baptism in 1742 and a marriage in 1758 it is more likely to be a late baptism (prove it!) or you've gone wrong.

Knowing what is likely and discounting what is unlikely is one of the quickest short cuts, but you have to get it right. One researcher told me a christian name could not possibly come from the mother's side of the family because men had control in those days (the 1720s) and would have chosen the children's names. Even if you go along with that (evidence, please?) why should a man not choose a name from his wife's family? Lots of people talk about family names being handed down and they turn out to be commonplace ones such as John, Henry and Mary. Certainly, particular names can be handed down and this is a useful clue; however, the English have no rules about a naming pattern compared with the strict rules of the Scots about who children shall be named after and the equally strict rule of some Jews that no child is to be named after a living relative.

How can you get it right? As regards both facts and attitudes there are a large number of social history books, both lightweight and heavyweight. Consider their opinions and look at their evidence. No expert *knows*; they are all drawing conclusions from their sources. The best sources are novels and letters of the time because of the unspoken assumptions, the throwaway remarks, the incidental descriptions of something taken for granted. However, novels are only reliable about their own time. Jane Austen is excellent (for the class she writes about) in the 1790s and Charles Dickens is excellent for the 1840s but Charles Dickens is no use to us when he writes about the French Revolution or the Gordon Riots. He had no more idea than we do about what it was really like 50 years before his time. The pre-war American South was not like *Gone With the Wind* (don't ask me what it was like).

This question of contemporaneity is an important one and I shall refer to it again in the section on Has It Been Done Before?

SUMMARY: Research the social background of your ancestors' lives to get an idea of what is probable/ possible/unlikely. The best sources for this were written at the time.

THE MAIN STAGES OF RESEARCH

Your relatives

All the how-to-do-it books tell you to start with the living family and this is true, but in the beginning they don't quite know what you want to know and actually you don't either. Go back to them when you have done some research. You may want to check some points or you may be able to jog their memories by telling them discoveries which they are confident are wrong. ('Don't be silly. Of course Grandpa wasn't from Birmingham – anyway his birthday was the same as my brother Frank's: that's why they named him after him.') New surnames may jog their memories ('I haven't thought of them for years,' or 'I was at school with one of them but I didn't know they were relatives'). Once you have uncovered the skeletons (Grandpa's illegitimacy, Uncle Frank's suicide . . .) they may be willing to fill you in on the details (or explain it away with their version of what really happened) when otherwise they weren't going to mention it at all.

Do make sure you ask all your relatives and compare their accounts. Everyone looks at things in a different way and your father's account of his relatives may be quite different from your mother's account of his relatives. One relative will understand Grandpa's job better because he was in the same line; another will know all the romantic history. One will give you simple, unimaginative facts, and another will have a fund of funny or affecting stories which show you what sort of people they were, yet not have the slightest knowledge or interest in what their birthdays were or whether they had children that died. One relative may have been brought up by an aunt or spent a lot of time with Grandma and so may know quite different things from the others and one of them (but which one?) may have been recovering from an illness and forced to stop in with the grown-ups one afternoon when all the other children went out to play. He was lying on the mat in front of the fire only half-listening but he was the only one to hear the story about Grandma's Grandma hiding the smuggled brandy under her voluminous skirts as the Customs men stopped them on Romney Marsh – your long-sought clue to where the family came from!

If your older relatives are dead do remember to ask your children. Family stories are usually passed from the old to the young and your parents may have told your children things which you never heard. Even your daughter-in-law may have been told by your mother many years ago how much she reminded her of Frank's sister Queenie that died or the girl my brother Jack was going to marry before he was killed on the Somme.

Be careful about believing what your relatives tell you. Apart from the sprinkling of liars and rogues in most families and the possibility that accounts are prejudiced by ancient squabbles, there is almost infinite scope for mistakes when people who are old now tell you what they think they heard when they were young from people who were old then talking about when they were young! The young misunderstand or the old leave out the unsuitable parts. The young ask silly questions and the old say, 'I wouldn't be surprised, dear,' because they don't want to spoil the child's fancy. 'Are we related to Nelson?' 'Might be, dear. You never know. Well, of course, everyone's related if you go back far enough.' Fifty years later your aunt can tell you, 'My grandma thought there might be a relationship with Lord Nelson . . .' and send you scurrying off to the *Dictionary of National Biography*. This can cut both ways: 'Are we related to Dr Crippen?' 'Certainly not. Eat your tea,' (meaning, 'Yes we are, but I'm not going to tell you.').

We often assume that in the past people have always lived in one place or followed the same trade or religion. Remembering where your grandparents lived when they were old is no

London Decr 22nd 1839

Mr Marlow

Sir I have great pleasure in
enclosing the Balance of your a/c
£1. 16. 0 and at same time tender
you my thanks for your kindness —
I should have transmitted it before this
but was in expectation of being in
London ere this — and am now merely
passing through for Brighton whither I
am going on Business — and think I
shall not have time to call at Richmond
this Route — I am happy to say I find
my Situation answer my Expectations
in every point — — and if you think.

Stories told by our relatives about the past are not always to be trusted, but old family letters and papers can sometimes confirm what seems unlikely. This otherwise unremarkable note dated 1839, proved a family tale about an ancestor in business in Leicester.

evidence as to where they had been born or spent their middle years. This applies even to your parents. ('You never told me we used to live in Finsbury Park.' 'Didn't I? Fancy you not knowing that. Your Dad had a job at the Arsenal just after the war.' 'What? The Royal Artillery?' 'No, you fool, the football ground. He was working for Emery's and they got the painting contract. Your school uniform came out of his bonus.') Most people's idea of 'always' means 'as far back as I remember and nobody ever told me any different'. This begs the question of whether they were a talkative family (and whether you paid attention if they did talk) and nowadays it carries us back to about 1920 which is nothing at all in our long, steady plod back to the 1500s. No ordinary family has more than one reliable tradition from before 1850.

A very common mistake is to assume Grandma's maiden name from the surname of relatives known to be on her side of the family, but Uncle Will Tomkins may have been her brother-in-law (or a nephew with a beard!) not her brother. Children think of everybody as old – if they think about it at all.

SUMMARY: Ask ALL your relatives. Check what they say!

Adoption

Family historians who were adopted begin in a special situation, though not necessarily a more difficult one than that of children of divorced parents or of people whose parents are dead or simply won't tell them anything.

Children often get a very false impression of what went on during a divorce or an adoption and the adults involved may have let off steam in the heat of the crisis and told them things which they wouldn't stand by once the situation has cooled down. In researching these episodes of a family history you have to make every effort to get information from somebody neutral who was an adult at the time. With illegitimacy too, other relatives may be much more reliable than either the child or the parents involved.

Since 1975 adopted children have been able to apply for access to their original birth record and since 1991 the Registrar

General has begun to operate an Adoption Contact register. Put simply, this allows birth parents and other relatives to assure an adopted person that contact would be welcome and to give a current address. Clearly the system is not compulsory and is in its early stages but it could offer reassurance to an adopted child who is wondering what sort of reception he or she will receive and it also gives a means of expression to families who would like to be contacted. One wonders whether a similar system could be developed for relatives who have lost contact through divorce.

A leaflet entitled *The Adoption Register* is available from St Catherine's House.

SUMMARY: Recent adoption is not necessarily a problem.

General Registration from 1837

It is unfortunate that in this hobby the most expensive part comes first. Most people cannot avoid buying a few civil registration certificates and people who try to cut corners here sometimes find they have built up a whole tree on a wrong first assumption, and that the tree they have built is someone else's, not their own. I myself have a neat little envelope marked 'Ancestors I Used to Have'.

In a straightforward ancestry one can usually get away with the birth and marriage certificate in each generation but if you cut corners even here you may never realise that Mary, wife of Thomas Robinson in the 1851 census (b Leeds about 1825), is not the same Mary Robinson, formerly Ackroyd, who appears on your ancestor's birth certificate in 1845. If your ancestor's mother died in 1846 aged 22 and the husband remarried another Mary in 1847 you may spend a long time looking for a Mary Ackroyd born at Leeds who never existed. Worse still, you may find one and cheerfully trace your Leeds ancestors when, if the real Mary Ackroyd could stand up, she would tell you she was from Sheffield. If there is the slightest doubt, buy some more certificates. Mary may be Maria or Mary Ann; Ackroyd may be Boothroyd or Ackerman or formerly Ackroyd, late Jones meaning that she had a first husband.

That said, there is no point spending money for the fun of it. If you have the time you may prefer to use the information on one birth certificate to trace your ancestor's baptism and then search through the church register picking out the brothers and sisters. Baptism entries quite often have the date of birth and an exact address. If the ancestors were nonconformists or Catholic you may get the mother's maiden name as well and with certain types of nonconformist register you get the grandfather's name, which is better than a GRO certificate and free into the bargain.

The same applies to marriages and deaths. Once you have located the entry in the GRO indexes you can search each of the likely churches or cemeteries for the right three-month period until you find the entry. One way takes time, the other takes money. You choose.

Either way the IHGS publishes maps of the registration districts of England and Wales for 1837 – 1851 and 1852 – 1946 and these are vital if you do not know the area from which your ancestors came or if it had a lot of registration districts, such as East Anglia. Otherwise it will be your plaintive voice which wafts over the counters at the FRC: 'Anyone know where Foleshill is, please?'

Now that the GRO indexes are available on microfiche and can be searched locally to you, it may hardly be worth your while to come up to London just to buy a couple of certificates. A number of Home Counties FHSs offer a courier service and will order certificates for you very cheaply. A number of professionals also advertise this service. Now that you can get the exact reference yourself this service is simple, reliable and very worthwhile. If you cannot do the search yourself the courier service is usually willing to do it for you. It costs a little more and you may have to let them decide which is the best entry to try first but then, if they are local and you aren't they may be better able to make a sensible choice. Find out if your local FHS has a regular arrangement or check the advertisements in *Family Tree Magazine*.

The local registrars may be more convenient if you live nearer and are quite sure of the area concerned. They are not usually so geared-up to family history enquiries as the GRO and reference numbers from the GRO indexes aren't usually applicable to local offices. They often charge for access and may be awkward about letting you see the records even then. However, if you get a certificate from the GRO and cannot read it the local registrar will nearly always interpret for you from his records and, being local, will not have the same difficulties with local place names or surnames as the clerk at the Family Records Centre. Provided they are still in existence that is; never expect local civil servants to have any historical knowledge. They might have but they don't have to have. If you want to know about something from 100 years ago ask at the Local Studies Library or the local museum.

Always allow for local spelling and pronunciation. Most of our ancestors did not spell their names at all so we are dependent on what a clerk could make of what he heard. It is meaningless to say your Clarke family always spelled the name with a final e. A name which is well known in its area may be miswritten or miscopied outside that area (the Maxteds of East Kent became McSteads when they got to America and descendants *knew* they must be Scottish). Bad handwriting may mean that a name is mistaken for something quite different and indexed in with it: Ferry/Terry; Burnett/Burnell; Bolton/Botton. The initial h and final g may come and go and names which contain a lot of short up-and-down strokes (minims) – u, i, m, n, v, w – may be miswritten almost every time they are copied. The letters r and s are often mistaken, especially at the end of a word, and carelessness makes the problem worse, for example Barton/Burton/Boston/Barlin . . . It's a wonder we find any of our ancestors. These problems are bad enough in a straightforward register or list; any index makes the matter worse. And things are no better nowadays.

The Department of Social Security can often help you to locate people who may still be alive through their national medical insurance records. Write to Special Section A, Room 101B, Department of Social Security, Records Branch, Newcastle-upon-Tyne, giving the full name and exact birth date if possible (but vaguer information may do if the name is uncommon), any known address and the last known

CERTIFIED COPY OF AN ENTRY OF DEATH

REGISTRATION DISTRICT Woodbridge

DEATH in the Sub-district of Woodbridge & Wilford

Columns:—	1	2	3	4	5	
No.	When and Where died	Name and surname	Sex	Age	Occupation	Cause
[illegible]	Twenty fourth May 1875 Woodbridge	John Milburn	Male	38 Years	Laborer	Accidental death injuries from [illegible] of a [illegible] [illegible]

CERTIFIED to be a true copy of an entry in the certified copy of a Register of Deaths in the District
Given at the GENERAL REGISTER OFFICE, LONDON, under the Seal of the said Office, the 4th

This certificate is issued in pursuance of the Births and Deaths Registration Act 19
sealed or stamped with the seal of the General Register Office shall be received as e
proof of the entry, and no certified copy purporting to have been given in the said O

DX 320699

CAUTION:—It is an offence to falsify a certificate or to make or genuine to the prejudice of any person, or to possess a

Form A504M Dd 8349771 20M 6/84 Mcr(304689)

Buying certificates is expensive, but sometimes it pays off. John Milburn's early death proved to have been the result of an accident and the certificate led to a report on the inquest in the local newspaper, with details of his family and where he worked.

marital status. Since the system was set up in 1948 they need to know a surname used after that date, which means they may not be able to help with an older woman if you do not know who she married. They will not tell you where she is but they will forward one letter from you to the person concerned if located

GIVEN AT THE GENERAL REGISTER OFFICE, LONDON

Application Number B28(62)

...d in the County of Suffolk

6	7	8	9
... of death	Signature, description and residence of informant	When registered	Signature of registrar
...rilad from ... received ... the bed ... Horse 6 days	Certificate received from Cooper & Brooks Coroner for the Liberty of Saint Etheldreda Inquest held 25th May 1875	Twenty fifth May 1875	William Arnott Registrar

... above mentioned.
day of February 1985

...53. Section 34 provides that any certified copy of an entry purporting to be ...vidence of the birth or death to which it relates without any further or other ...ffice shall be of any force or effect unless it is sealed or stamped as aforesaid.

...knowingly use a false certificate or a copy of a false certificate intending it to be accepted as ...certificate knowing it to be false without lawful authority.

and this letter gives the person concerned the freedom to decide whether he or she wishes to be found. A leaflet about this service is available from St Catherine's House.

I have already referred in passing to the fact that the early GRO indexes are now available for sale on microfiche. The SoG has a full set of birth, marriage and death indexes to 1920 and this means not only that you can avoid the weight of the heavy volumes and sit down to work but you can use them on Saturdays and the SoG late-opening evenings. Sets of these microfiches are becoming steadily more available and your local FHS and Local Studies Library should know the nearest one to you.

Even if you are rich you may not want to buy every possible certificate from the GRO. I have already referred to using mid-19th century baptism registers to document your ancestors' brothers and sisters; this is even more valuable as regards Anglican marriages where the information given is exactly the same. However, it may not work so well as regards deaths since most city churches ceased to bury in their own churchyards soon after 1853 and you will need to check the possible borough or private cemeteries, many of which have no indexes, will not allow public access and will not search a period as long as three months. For London, the SoG has published *Greater London Cemeteries and Crematoria and their Records* which details all the possible places of burial arranged by area and in date order. This can be used in conjunction with the West Surrey FHS Research Aid No. 6, *Guide to Genealogical Research in Victorian London* (there is a similar booklet for Edwardian London) which gives a list of the Victorian parish churches in each registration district with a note of where they are and the date their registers begin. You can spend £6 at the GRO or a couple of hours at the LMA. Either way will probably produce the information. You choose.

Indexes for Scottish civil registration are held at New Register House, Edinburgh but microfilm copies of these indexes from 1855 (when they began) to 1920 are at the SoG which also has microfilms of the full certificates for 1855. Better still, the new computerised indexes, 1855 to date, are available on CD-ROM at the Family Records Centre. There is a small charge for use, at present £4 for half an hour. If you can get to London more easily than Edinburgh you may be able to do all your index searching at the Society and save your valuable time in Edinburgh for actually looking up things in the original registers – a possibility which does not exist in England or Wales. The Scottish IGI has also indexed all entries to 1875 though these indexes are county-wide not country-wide.

Microfilm copies of the Irish central indexes of Births, Marriages and Deaths are held at the (Mormon) Hyde Park Family History Centre (see Appendix). They would be available on request at any other local Mormon Family History Centre (see last section).

SUMMARY: You will have to buy some GRO certificates at £6. Don't cut corners here or your research may go wrong at the very beginning. You may be able to get the same information for free at the CRO. Use local people for local knowledge. Beware of spelling and handwriting; almost any variant can occur occasionally. The DSS can help with locating living people. Some Scottish and Irish material is available in England, especially in London.

The census

Microfilms of every census for the period 1841 – 1891 for the whole of England, Wales, Channel Islands and the Isle of Man are available on open access at the Family Records Centre; most county record offices and local studies libraries now have the ones for their own areas. An FFHS booklet, *Census Returns on Microfilm*, gives full details. Certain information about named individuals is available from the 1901 census and a leaflet about this service is available from the FRC. The charge is equivalent to about three certificates and if you are stuck with an ancestor's age or birthplace this may be the only way forward. Remember that it is every bit as useful for an 80 year old as for a three year old but you must be able to provide an exact address (even in a village).

No complete set of the Scottish census is available south of the border but individual reels can be bought and the SoG is steadily building up a collection. If you cannot easily get to Edinburgh you may like to use the SoG sponsorship scheme to get access to the reels you need (see later section).

Generally speaking, Irish census material has not survived

and the only 19th century substitute is Sir Richard Griffith's *Primary Land Valuation 1848–1864* which details all the occupiers of land and is name indexed by county. Copies on microfiche are available at the British Library (official publications section), the SoG and an increasing number of larger local studies libraries where researcher interest has justified the expense.

To balance the loss of earlier material, the Irish censuses of 1901 and 1911 are open and a project has begun to index them. To date only Longford, Tyrone and Fermanagh are available but more are in the pipeline.

A large number of FHSs have indexed census returns for their areas, mostly concentrating on the 1851 census and moving on to others only when they have finished that. Full details of what is available can be found in *Marriage, Census and other Indexes*, another FFHS publication on your local FHS bookstall. In addition, the Genealogical Society of Utah and the FFHS have organised a national project to index the 1881 census. County indexes are now available and a national index is expected soon. Watch for news in *Family Tree Magazine*.

As family historians we have a natural tendency to talk about where the family was living at a given date, but a large number of people spent years away from their family – if they had one. Servants, apprentices, farm workers, soldiers and sailors had all left home by 12 or 14 and if they left the area they would have had little or no contact with their parents again and even less contact with their other relatives if their parents were dead or remarried. With no telephone, no holidays, little transport or post and no spare money to pay for them, no facility in writing and nothing particular to say, how could it have been different? We look at two-up, two-down cottages (one-up, one-down if they're old enough) and we ask how on earth they managed to bring up all those children there. The answer of course is that they didn't, not all at the same time. The oldest children had long since left home by the time the youngest were born and even when they were younger, parents with half a dozen children were only too glad to let one go to a sister or neighbour with love to spare and no children of her own. A child adopted in this way might have the chance of a better life as an only child in a more comfortable home. However, there was no formal procedure for adoption until 1927. All adoptions before that date were informal and direct evidence is very unusual. However, if a child was boarded out from a workhouse or orphanage or similar institution, then there may be very detailed records.

As regards adults, a great many people would have just happened to be away from home on census nights: coastguards, commercial travellers, policemen and bakers on night-shift, male servants sleeping in while their families are in the mews or down in the village, single mothers in servants' attics while their children are living with the grandparents, people in the building trades moving from one job to another; even our settled ancestors in the towns were on a week's notice given or received and would move easily as their family expanded or contracted (as it did most years!), as they got a job a bit further away, as they got a better job and could afford another room, or lost their job and had to take a basement or share facilities. In the poorer areas of London a lot of families paid for their lodgings by the night and dozed in the street if they couldn't find the necessary. For these people it was even easier to move as they lived from hand to mouth and had almost no possessions. Country people did not move so often, but until bicycles became common, farmworkers had to live near their work and if they moved to a new farm then they moved to a new cottage. Thank God for indexes!

SUMMARY: Local censuses are widely available and widely indexed. Many people were not part of a family or were away from home on census night. Everybody moved far more often than we think (though not necessarily very far).

Indexes – a two-edged sword

When we find an index to a large source we tend to breathe a sigh of relief: now we can check in two minutes what might otherwise take us two days. You can see the efficient, muscular people at the Family Records Centre or in the Wills section at Somerset House. They chug rhythmically along the shelves:

BASH! flick, skim, slam. BASH! flick, skim, slam – nobody I want there! People who are browsing often work along the likely books on a shelf without even noticing what they have looked at. This approach can work if you are looking for a specific, recognisable entry – and find it. However, it is important to remember that an index is worse as well as better than the original.

The index itself may be partial, omitting, say, 'mere' lists of names in the Appendix (the very thing that interests us). Even if it is complete it has introduced new errors of transcription and interpretation and it has destroyed the clues of context by which we convince ourselves that *in this case* Thomas and Ann Barton are the same as Thomas and Anne Burton and that actually *in this case* even Thomas and Hannah Burton are the same couple. A good index will give cross-references or index doubtful names under all the alternatives. If the index was compiled by someone with good local knowledge and flair then it may make decisions you can trust (any Gandy in the south-west is probably a Candy but any Candy in the north-west is probably a Gandy). If the transcript was done by someone without local knowledge and the index was computer-generated then even if it is accurate it won't be helpful, and it may not even be accurate.

The moral, I'm afraid, is that you must never just check an index. You must look at the beginning of the index to see if it sets any limits and you must look at the title page and the foreword to see what is actually being dealt with. The short title may sin by omission. Thus *Middlesex Protestation Returns 1641* turns out to be a transcript of the surviving material and your ancestors are not listed because no material has survived for the parishes they were probably in. Dumfriesshire MIs – pre-1855 inscriptions – may mean a complete transcript of any stone which starts before 1855 or only pre-1855 entries with later entries omitted and no note of whether there were any. The foreword explains; the index and the title page don't.

SUMMARY: Indexes make searching quicker but they introduce new errors and destroy the clues of context. Always read the introduction to an index to see what it actually covers.

Strays indexes

Naturally, in checking for our ancestors we check the likely area thoroughly and notice numbers, sometimes large numbers, of people from miles away. 'If someone's looking for him they'll never find him', we tell ourselves and realise that our Kent man may have married in Cornwall and our bricklayer from Manchester may have died while rebuilding Folkestone harbour. Most FHSs have now set up a strays index to bring together references to people from their area who had moved away whether temporarily or permanently. These are random entries sent in by kind people (such as you) who see an interesting reference and take the time to jot it on to a 5x3 inch slip of paper and send it to the Strays Co-ordinator of their own or another society.

There are also some systematic extracts: for example, an index of everyone in Liverpool in 1851 who gave a birthplace in Cumbria and another of everyone in London, the Home Counties and East Anglia who gave a birthplace in Kent. This latter includes vast numbers of young servants and shopmen, gentry and artisans, paupers, lodgers and sailors who were from Kent but no longer living there and it also contains hundreds of references to persons who were not Kentish in origin but had been in the Services and had a child born at Chatham, Greenwich, Woolwich or Sheerness. If you have a particular problem with army or navy ancestry this index just may hold the solution.

The 1881 census indexes produced by the Mormons have an index of strays as standard.

The FHSS booklet *Marriage, Census and other Indexes* in the series of Gibson Guides has a title which is self-explanatory and is worth its weight in gold. I think if you were only going to use one helpful booklet out of the wide range available this would be it.

Now that so many indexes are fed on to computers it is easy to generate these lists sorted by birthplace (though the machine won't pick up errors). This can make it possible to look for people who gave the same birthplace as your ancestor and may

be related by blood or friendship – or have become so. Your earliest ancestor in an area may in fact have come to an uncle or cousin of a surname you wouldn't recognise yet, or may have come to the area because the local landowner back home was encouraging surplus workers to go to his brother-in-law's factories in the north. If a lot of people in the area had come from the same place then perhaps your ancestor who died before the 1851 census was also from there. This can work both ways: some people run a mile from any reminder of back home and are too excited by the new to want to talk about the old. It has often been said of the American immigrant families who have now become prosperous and suburban that this generation is working hard to remember what its parents worked hard to forget. People who were closer to poverty, servitude, dirt and perhaps foreignness didn't have our rose-coloured spectacles. (This does not apply to your ancestors who were all warm, caring individuals who were kind to animals and deeply respected by their community. Above all they smelled nice!)
SUMMARY: Most family history societies now have a strays index. These and many other useful indexes are listed in *Marriage, Census and Other Indexes* (a Gibson Guide published by the FFHS).

Maps and directories

Family history without maps is like painting with your eyes shut. Even if you know personally the areas from which your ancestors came they will certainly be different now from what they were 50 years ago, let alone one or two hundred. Ideally you need the following:
– the modern Ordnance Survey map for when you visit the area.
– for cities: a map of how it was between the industrial growth which had mostly taken place by the 1850s and the enormous changes which have taken place since 1930. The best general series is published by Alan Godfrey Maps who are expanding the range as fast as demand justifies. Available

through the SoG and the local FHS.

– for towns: many 19th century maps have been produced by libraries or local history societies and are for sale fairly cheaply. The Guildhall Library sells an excellent reprint of *Stanford's Map of London* 1862, and a series of maps called An A to Z of (Elizabethan, Restoration, Georgian, Regency, Victorian) London. Booth's map of 1889 assigns every street a colour depending on the general social level of the inhabitants from yellow for the upper crust in Mayfair down to black in Whitechapel and nearby for the vicious and semi-criminal. At present it is out of print, but hopefully for a short time only. The local FHS should know what to recommend.

– for villages and the countryside: a reprint of the First Ordnance Survey has been produced by David and Charles, Newton Abbot, Devon. Each map has a different date, but clearly marked on it. They cover the whole of England and Wales (not Scotland or Ireland) in 97 maps and are excellent for showing how the hamlets and villages relate to each other and the growing towns which later swallowed them. The roads, rivers, bridges and hills help us to see how travel was easy in some directions and impossible in others; we can work out which market towns our ancestors used not just for buying and selling but for marriages by licence and the annual hiring fair which often still determined where they would live for the following year.

There is a steady programme to publish these volumes in hard-back volumes covering two or three counties each.

There is often no published large-scale map of a village and you must try to find a hand-written one such as those often drawn up for enclosure or tithe commutation. In the 18th century they might be part of a glebe terrier; manor court rolls and estate papers often include them. Study them carefully and it may be possible to have a photocopy but don't trace them unless you are very skilful *and* are going to publish them so that your work is a conservation exercise. Old documents won't bear a lot of handling and if two or three amateurs each produce a bit of scrap which they throw away within six months then the document will have been destroyed for nothing. Exercise

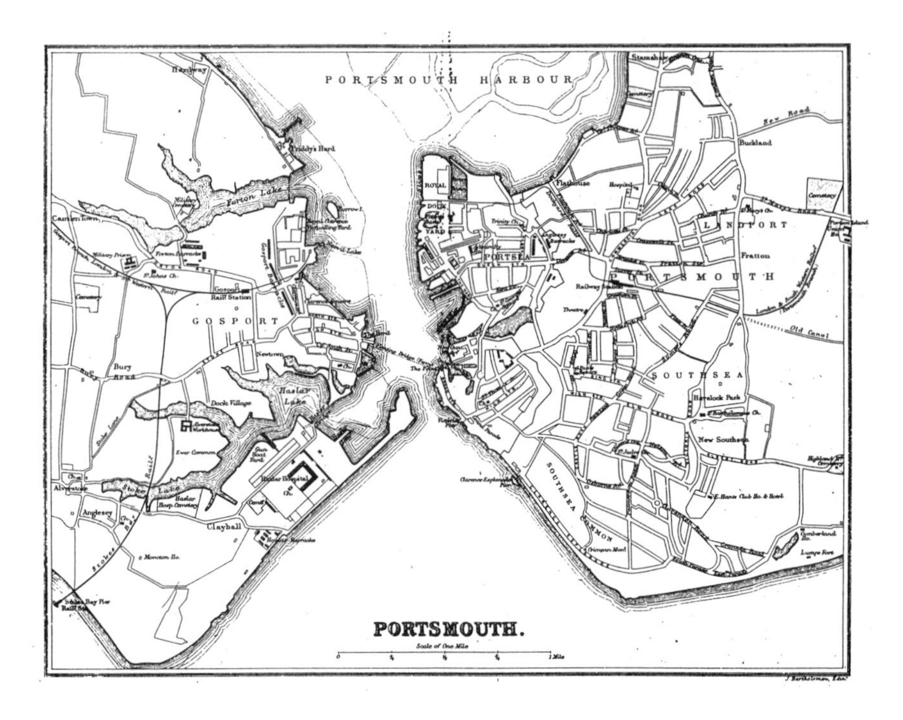

Maps are an essential aid to research. As well as the usual sources, keep an eye open for maps published in contemporary guides, such as this map of Portsmouth from the 1874 edition of Black's Picturesque Tourist of England.

self-restraint.

There are a number of excellent reprints of 18th century county maps, many of them published in association with Harry Margary of Lympne Castle, Kent. Some were produced by subscription and were never on general sale – others are now out of print and could be re-issued if there were sufficient demand. A few were subsidised; most are quality productions at a coffee-table price. None the less useful and a pleasure to own, but you may have to check with your bank manager first.

At a more technical level, I have already referred to maps of registration districts produced by the IHGS. They have also produced parish maps covering every county in England, Wales and Scotland. These show all the C of E parishes to 1837 with chapels of ease where relevant and the date of the first entry in the register. They are coloured to show the Diocesan boundaries and note any peculiar jurisdictions for the proving of wills. If you are interested in enough counties to justify the expense, the whole English and Welsh series is available bound with another set of county maps (from 1834), a separate index and grid reference for each county and useful information about which registers are deposited centrally or on the IGI (C.R. Humphery-Smith (Ed.), *The Phillimore Atlas and Index of Parish Registers*, 1995.)

Access to a good gazetteer is essential for the family historian. Our ancestors' places of birth, marriage and death may get garbled in the records like our ancestors' surnames; on other occasions they may cite a farm or tiny hamlet which is very difficult to locate or may not exist nowadays as a separate entity. Sometimes only local knowledge will do; who would guess that Trosley in Kent is actually spelt Trottescliffe? The SoG is in Clerkenwell but in talking about it you might say near Old Street or near Barbican (depending which Underground station you use), or over in the City if you had thought they were still in South Kensington (and we used to call that Gloucester Road!). In terms of London Boroughs it is in Islington but that is the least useful description of all since the Borough covers a dozen separate areas, each with its own name and identity.

Sometimes neither map nor gazetteer will help. In most towns people describe their area in terms of landmarks: churches, hospitals, gas works, war memorials, above all pubs and these names are often enshrined in bus stops and railway stations. The Great North Road out of London ran from the Angel past the Nags Head and the Archway up to the Bald-Faced Stag, out to Tally Ho and on up to the Red Lion after which you were in Hertfordshire. Anyone local will find no difficulty with that but from a distance you need a directory. The modern form of telephone directory or Yellow Pages is not much use. We need the old form which set out the streets and noted exactly where the institutions and side streets were. Most local libraries have some for their area; the SoG, the Guildhall Library and the British Library have excellent national collections. Quite a lot have been reprinted and can be bought for use at a distance.

A contemporary directory complements a map (which simply tells us what there was) by giving us clues as to what people felt there was, what they felt was their local market, hospital, church, park, theatre. If your ancestors were small tradesmen or farmers it will tell you who else was in their line of work: a guide to who they socialised with. This may sound as if I have moved into social history and further away from the tree but

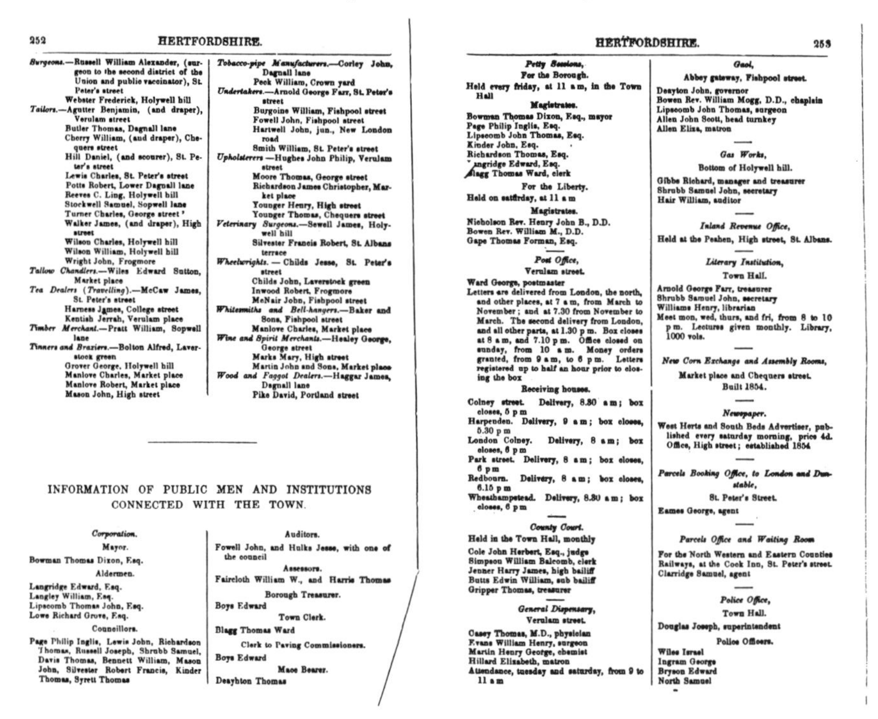

252 HERTFORDSHIRE.

Surgeons.—Russell William Alexander, (surgeon to the second district of the Union and public vaccinator), St. Peter's street
Webster Frederick, Holywell hill
Tailors.—Agutter Benjamin, (and draper), Verulam street
Butler Thomas, Dagnall lane
Cherry William, (and draper), Chequers street
Hill Daniel, (and scourer), St. Peter's street
Lewis Charles, St. Peter's street
Potts Robert, Lower Dagnall lane
Reeves C. Ling, Holywell hill
Stockwell Samuel, Sopwell lane
Turner Charles, George street
Walker James, (and draper), High street
Wilson Charles, Holywell hill
Wilson William, Holywell hill
Wright John, Frogmore
Tallow Chandlers.—Wiles Edward Sutton, Market place
Tea Dealers (Travelling).—McCaw James, St. Peter's street
Harness James, College street
Kentish Jerrah, Verulam place
Timber Merchant.—Pratt William, Sopwell lane
Tinners and Braziers.—Bolton Alfred, Laverstock green
Grover George, Holywell hill
Manlove Charles, Market place
Manlove Robert, Market place
Mason John, High street
Tobacco-pipe Manufacturers.—Corley John, Dagnall lane
Peck William, Crown yard
Undertakers.—Arnold George Farr, St. Peter's street
Burgoine William, Fishpool street
Fowell John, Fishpool street
Hartwell John, jun., New London road
Smith William, St. Peter's street
Upholsterers.—Hughes John Philip, Verulam street
Moore Thomas, George street
Richardson James Christopher, Market place
Younger Henry, High street
Younger Thomas, Chequers street
Veterinary Surgeons.—Sewell James, Holywell hill
Silvester Francis Robert, St. Albans terrace
Wheelwrights.—Childs Jesse, St. Peter's street
Childs John, Laverstock green
Inwood Robert, Frogmore
McNair John, Fishpool street
Whitesmiths and Bell-hangers.—Baker and Sons, Fishpool street
Manlove Charles, Market place
Wine and Spirit Merchants.—Healey George, George street
Marks Mary, High street
Martin John and Sons, Market place
Wood and Faggot Dealers.—Haggar James, Dagnall lane
Pike David, Portland street

INFORMATION OF PUBLIC MEN AND INSTITUTIONS CONNECTED WITH THE TOWN.

Corporation.

Mayor.

Bowman Thomas Dixon, Esq.

Aldermen.

Langridge Edward, Esq.
Langley William, Esq.
Lipscomb Thomas John, Esq.
Lowe Richard Grove, Esq.

Councillors.

Page Philip Inglis, Lewis John, Richardson Thomas, Russell Joseph, Shrubb Samuel, Davis Thomas, Bennett William, Mason John, Silvester Robert Francis, Kinder Thomas, Syrett Thomas

Auditors.

Fowell John, and Hulks Jesse, with one of the council

Assessors.

Faircloth William W., and Harris Thomas

Borough Treasurer.

Boys Edward

Town Clerk.

Blagg Thomas Ward

Clerk to Paving Commissioners.

Boys Edward

Mace Bearer.

Deayhton Thomas

HERTFORDSHIRE. 253

Petty Sessions,

For the Borough.

Held every friday, at 11 a m, in the Town Hall

Magistrates.

Bowman Thomas Dixon, Esq., mayor
Page Philip Inglis, Esq.
Lipscomb John Thomas, Esq.
Kinder John, Esq.
Richardson Thomas, Esq.
Langridge Edward, Esq.
Blagg Thomas Ward, clerk

For the Liberty.

Held on saturday, at 11 a m

Magistrates.

Nicholson Rev. Henry John B., D.D.
Bowen Rev. William M., D.D.
Gape Thomas Forman, Esq.

Post Office,

Verulam street.

Ward George, postmaster
Letters are delivered from London, the north, and other places, at 7 a m, from March to November; and at 7.30 from November to March. The second delivery from London, and all other parts, at 1.30 p m. Box closes at 8 a m, and 7.10 p m. Office closed on sunday, from 10 a m. Money orders granted, from 9 a m, to 6 p m. Letters registered up to half an hour prior to closing the box

Receiving houses.

Colney street. Delivery, 8.30 a m; box closes, 5 p m
Harpenden. Delivery, 9 a m; box closes, 5.30 p m
London Colney. Delivery, 8 a m; box closes, 6 p m
Park street. Delivery, 8 a m; box closes, 6 p m
Redbourn. Delivery, 8 a m; box closes, 6.15 p m
Wheathampstead. Delivery, 8.30 a m; box closes, 6 p m

County Court.

Held in the Town Hall, monthly

Cole John Herbert, Esq., judge
Simpson William Balcomb, clerk
Jenner Harry James, high bailiff
Butts Edwin William, sub bailiff
Gripper Thomas, treasurer

General Dispensary,

Verulam street.

Casey Thomas, M.D., physician
Evans William Henry, surgeon
Martin Henry George, chemist
Hillard Elizabeth, matron
Attendance, tuesday and saturday, from 9 to 11 a m

Gaol,

Abbey gateway, Fishpool street.

Deayton John, governor
Bowen Rev. William Mogg, D.D., chaplain
Lipscomb John Thomas, surgeon
Allen John Scott, head turnkey
Allen Eliza, matron

Gas Works,

Bottom of Holywell hill.

Gibbs Richard, manager and treasurer
Shrubb Samuel John, secretary
Hair William, auditor

Inland Revenue Office,

Held at the Peahen, High street, St. Albans.

Literary Institution,

Town Hall.

Arnold George Farr, treasurer
Shrubb Samuel John, secretary
Williams Henry, librarian
Meet mon, wed, thurs, and fri, from 8 to 10 p m. Lectures given monthly. Library, 1000 vols.

New Corn Exchange and Assembly Rooms,

Market place and Chequers street.
Built 1854.

Newspaper.

West Herts and South Beds Advertiser, published every saturday morning, price 4d. Office, High street; established 1854

Parcels Booking Office, to London and Dunstable,

St. Peter's Street.

Eames George, agent

Parcels Office and Waiting Room

For the North Western and Eastern Counties Railways, at the Cock Inn, St. Peter's street.
Clarridge Samuel, agent

Police Office,

Town Hall.

Douglas Joseph, superintendent

Police Officers.

Wiles Israel
Ingram George
Bryson Edward
North Samuel

Pigot & Co's Directory of Hertfordshire published in 1833 gives a list not only of businesses and trades, but also 'public men and institutions' connected in this case with St Albans. Contemporary directories complement maps and help to create a 'snapshot' picture of a local community.

where children were growing up in the business they were more likely to marry amongst the children of their parents' business friends.

Another useful clue can be found in bus and tram routes. Once people began to move out of the centre they naturally looked for ease of access to work or each other and they moved out to a place where accessible housing suited their pocket. Later their circumstances may have changed but initially that was the reason. When we were moving out 20 years ago we tied ourselves to the bus route which happened to link where I worked and where my mother-in-law lived. We ignored the areas we didn't like or couldn't afford and also the one that was hilly as that would be bad for my mother-in-law. Twenty years later I have long since changed jobs and mother-in-law has died but we still live within 100 yards of the original house we chose. In a similar way my wife's grandparents can be shown to have simply moved out along the tram route from where he worked to the point where new houses for their type of person were being built about 1900. Not everybody remembers to ask *why* their ancestors lived where they did.

SUMMARY: A great many old maps have now been reprinted. Old directories help you get a feel for what the area was like. Consider *why* your ancestors lived where they did.

Monumental inscriptions

For at least 30 years there has been a series of five year plans (initiated by the IHGS) to copy every monumental inscription in the country and a vast amount of work has been done. In many counties the country churchyards are now almost completely transcribed and a lot of work has also been done on non-conformist grounds. Copies are often on microfiche and for sale. Details are available either through the local FHS, the FFHS *Current Publications by Member Societies* (two series: one for booklets and one for microfiches) or through the SoG *Monumental Inscriptions in the Library of the Society of Genealogists* (in two parts). Clearly an indexed transcript can save both time and effort, though the usual warnings about indexes and transcripts apply and the gravestone you want just might be there even if the copy you look at doesn't include it.

Inscriptions, where found, are clearly an excellent and reliable short cut to death dates. They save money on certificates and may point you to people or sources you had never thought of ('Also their son Thomas who died in New Zealand'). Moreover, not only are there often a number of names on the same stone with the relationship stated but related family groups often have plots near each other in the churchyard. This even applies in borough cemeteries where plots are more regimented: a dozen or so related Gandy graves are all on the same small triangle of ground in Warrington Public Cemetery and for all I know some of the other plots on the same triangle may turn out to be other cousins or relatives of the in-laws.

Unfortunately not all our ancestors are in sweet little English country churchyards. In the towns, space was at a premium and bodies had to be packed in tight-to-bursting patches of ground which had to be used over and over again; there was no question of a stone for most people and once the fashion for them spread amongst the middle classes they began to campaign to be buried elsewhere. In London the great private cemeteries at Abney Park, Highgate, Kensal Green, Norwood, Tower Hamlets, Brompton and Brookwood were opened in the 1830s and provided decent burial which was increasingly impossible in City churches. After 1853 most parishes bought a huge plot of land out in the country (as it then was) and those who could afford it could begin to put up permanent monuments.

Meanwhile, in the centre, such stones as there were became increasingly subject to pollution and destruction; as people moved out the graves were less and less tended and a combination of bombing and inner-city renewal (ie knocking the old stuff down) has put paid to most of them.

There are thus two problems, both equally serious for family historians. In the town centres fewer stones were put up in the first place and fewer still survived, while in the spacious new cemeteries there are too many stones (sometimes wildly overgrown) for the researcher to be able to browse with any

Gravestones may prove a short cut to finding death dates and relationships – if you can find them. As churchyards filled, many towns opened new cemeteries from the mid 19th century on. This plot, pictured in the 1920s and now considerably fuller, is at Woodbridge in Suffolk.

hope of success. There are always excellent records, but they are nearly always arranged by date or plot number and may have no index to names. Thus, in the country, gravestones can be used as a short cut to deaths; in the towns you have to locate and buy your GRO certificates in order to start looking for a gravestone.

In Scotland there is an additional problem. The pure Presbyterian church objected to gravestones and, except for the anglicised upper classes, early stones are uncommon. However, when the fashion spread north, a lot of gravestones were put up retrospectively. These may refer to deaths which took place donkey's years before the erection of the stone, so how reliable are they? In England you could check against the burial registers, but most Presbyterian churches have no burial

registers, so the stone may be the only evidence there is. However, it is not contemporary evidence.
SUMMARY: MIs give information which is almost always reliable. In the country they can be easy to find; much less so in the towns.

Wills

From 1858 indexes of all wills in England and Wales are centralised at Somerset House. Copies of these are now available on microfilm; SoG has copies of them all to 1930 and no doubt other repositories will acquire them. These indexes give much more information than those of the GRO and are much quicker to search, so that if your ancestor may have left a will this is a better way to locate it and his death than starting at St Catherine's House. If your ancestor is unlikely to have left a will but has a fairly common name then check your list of possible deaths against the will indexes to see who you can eliminate before starting to buy certificates.

Wills contain firm and reliable statements of relationship and you should try every possibility for people who may mention your ancestors: godparents, neighbours, employers, in-laws through wives you are not descended from, people they owed money to or people who owed money to them, people of the same religion or living in the same area if this is practicable. If your ancestors were Quakers or corn-chandlers or lived in a small community then almost anyone of the same type may have mentioned them. Equals may appoint each other as executor or give details of business arrangements or debts to be cancelled if their children marry: social superiors may leave small sums of money amongst a whole range of dependants. A vicar may mention godchildren amongst the labourers. A lady may mention her servants and ex-servants. Searching all these wills may not sound like a short cut but any one of them may contain the vital clue ('now of Oswestry') or some such cast-iron piece of proof.

The same applies to searching wills of related surnames outside the area. You know where your ancestors were but you

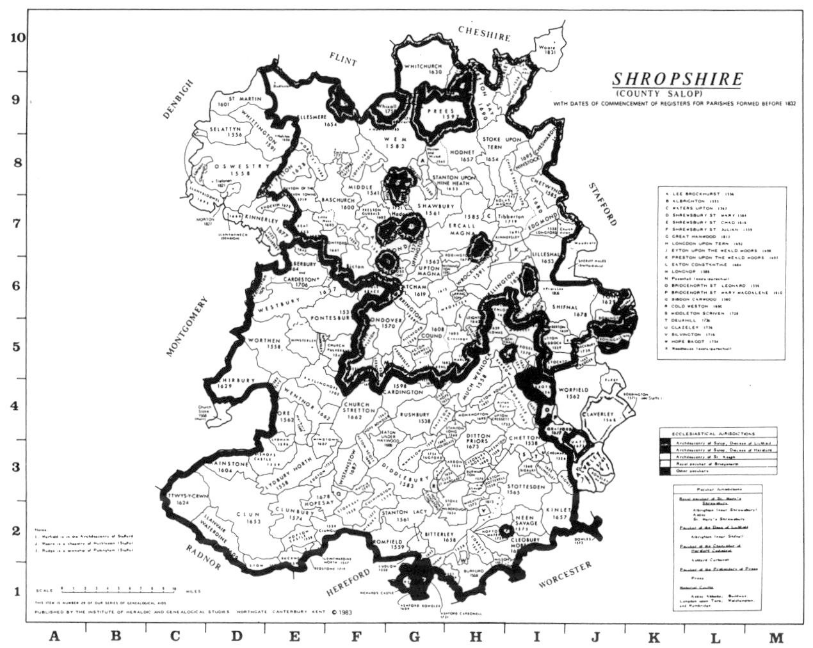

*The county maps produced by the Institute of Heraldic and Genealogical Studies show ecclesiastical jurisdictions as well as parishes, invaluable if you are searching for a will before 1858. (*The Phillimore Atlas and Index of Parish Registers *has a full set.)*

don't know for certain (yet) where they came from and you don't know where all their uncles and aunts and cousins had gone to. The proof that Thomas is the son of James may lie in the will of Edward who is a cousin or nephew living 50 miles away and dying 50 years later. The proof that the family came from Derby may be in the mention of some painting by a great-grandson in Worthing. Researchers are often in a hurry to trace backwards and think that the cousins can be left until later but you can't tell which of your ancestors meant most to each other and may have been linked. When her husband died my grandma bought a two-plot grave intending to be buried with him in due course. Thirty years later she let one of her sisters have the plot to bury her son who had died in his fifties and she herself was cremated another dozen years later. The nephew was brought up in France and his uncle died when he was ten, so the two people on that stone may never have met and certainly cannot have known each other well. The two sisters who link them are recorded somewhere else entirely.

Of course, part of our problem in tracing movement is that the vital clue which proves the connection is probably in the original home area and we don't know where that was yet. Catch 22 – but at least when you have gone the long way round and produced a likely hypothesis some firm piece of evidence appears and proves it. Family history wouldn't be fun if it were too easy!

Referring to the wills of employers highlights the fact that our ancestors often moved for reasons that had nothing to do with their own family at all. When Mr Jones marries Miss Smith (with £30,000) the new lady of the manor will bring her own lady's maid with her. Until she puts down roots in the new area she is likely to ask her mother or elder sisters when she needs a reliable nurse or cook and so within a couple of years of her arrival a number of single women will have been imported into the parish. If you can't find where your servant ancestress came from try looking where the local gentry had their connections. The personal letters or diaries of Lady Mary may even prove the move. The same applies to specialist groups such as Quakers, Catholics, Huguenots and Jews who would sooner marry or find servants from 50 miles away than link up with an outsider from next door.

In the period before 1858 there were over 300 courts which might have proved the will of your ancestor and kept a copy of it. The jurisdictions are all detailed on the IHGS parish maps which I have already recommended and in practice if you know where your ancestor probably died then there are only three or four courts to search. Yet another of the marvellous FFHS Gibson Guides (*Probate Jurisdiction – Where to Look for Wills*) gives full details of local holdings, dates, gaps, availability and is another must.

From 1796 the Inland Revenue returns at the PRO bring together details of most (not all) wills in the country. These returns are now at the Family Records Centre and a leaflet is obtainable from the PRO.

In former times, when parish registers were much less easy to get at and there was less interest in tracing labouring families, wills were the prime source in genealogy and many old trees are based almost entirely on them. There are calendars or indexes to the wills of almost every county to at least 1700 and often to 1858: these are usually in print but may otherwise be in card index or similar form at the CRO. SoG has an almost complete set of indexes for the whole country in one form or another. Remember that some indexes are only calendars – arrangement by first letter only, often in date order within that letter. You cannot just flick to Clark but have to search all the Cs. Still, much better than nothing.

In some cases full abstracts of wills for certain areas have been published. These are always worth trying even if they are not from the area where you would have expected to find your ancestors. Essex has a marvellous 16th century series and Lancashire has a good series of gentry wills published by the Chetham Society. The London Recusant has published a good series for priests and middle class Catholics (don't disregard them because they are priests – they are archetypal single uncles and very inclined to leave small amounts of money round all their nephews and nieces.

There are a great many similar groups of abstracts for particular parishes – ask the FHS; these are more likely to be in local history sources than family history ones.

SUMMARY: From 1858 all wills are indexed centrally at Somerset House; before 1858 use the FFHS Gibson Guide *Probate Jurisdictions* to decide where best to look. Try wills of people of the same trade or religion or even the same village, not just those of the same surname.

Parish registers and nonconformists

Before the mid-19th century, parish registers are our usual source for evidence about our ancestors' baptisms, marriages and burials. Most of them are centralised in county or city record offices; there are a large number of transcripts, a great many of which have been microfilmed or microfiched and can be bought or borrowed, and the best national collection in the UK is in the SoG library, which operates a postal loan service on many items for members. Checking registers is getting easier and easier and the steady growth of the Mormon IGI (see later) means that finding possible entries to check out is getting easier and easier too.

However, if you live near London or if the register you want is only available locally or not available at all (there is a technical name for the law by which this always happens to you) then why not try nonconformist possibilities first. Apart from Catholics the vast majority of pre-1837 nonconformist registers are deposited at the PRO. The originals can be seen there but the whole series has also been microfilmed and many county record offices and local studies libraries now have the ones which relate to their areas. The entries have also been fed onto the IGI.

The registers available include not only those of the main denominations but also those of Dr Williams's Library and the Wesleyan Methodist Registry, both of which recorded the births of families from all over the country. (Ruth Killon has extracted all the Kent, Derbyshire, Gloucestershire and Shropshire births from Dr Williams's Library and Vicky Uffindell has done the same for Cambridgeshire.) The burials at Bunhill Fields include the majority of London nonconformists; the Fleet registers contain irregular marriages of vast numbers of ordinary people (not just a few select gentry as is often supposed); and the lying-in hospitals are the first maternity hospitals and began the work of reducing perinatal mortality. A most useful extract (by Stephen Hale) of Kent, Surrey and Sussex entries from the Fleet registers is at SoG, which also has complete transcripts of the nonconformist registers for some counties (Cornwall, Surrey,

Sussex, rural Middlesex and Shropshire, to my knowledge) as well as parts of others.

Note that the class-list is concerned with baptisms, marriages and burials but that many of the volumes contain other material such as confirmations or a list of the congregation. Always check the class-list as well as the microfilm as unfortunately not all the material was filmed; when the main bulk of a volume had been copied, a few isolated pages in the middle or at the end could easily be overlooked.

Researchers are usually aware that between 1754 and 1837 legal marriages could only take place in the Church of England except in the case of Quakers and Jews (there are registers from both groups in the PRO). However, Catholics certainly continued to perform their own marriages and many marriage entries survive. For the marriage to have been legal there should have been a second ceremony in the C of E (and there probably was) but the Catholic entry may give different information and is well worth chasing. Continental priests brought with them the registration customs of countries such as Belgium and France where civil registration was introduced earlier than here and a Catholic marriage entry may well give the place of birth, the names of the mothers (with maiden names) as well as the fathers and even the places that the parents lived. This is gold dust if you are stuck with ancestors for whom the English census just says 'born Ireland'.

However, here again social history comes into play. Under Providence, religion is very much a question of social class. The real labouring poor were obliged to be Church of England to be certain of the poor relief which they were all going to need and the professional and upper classes needed to be Church of England to go to the universities, enter the professions or the services or take any part in public life. The appointment of local clergy was often in the hands of the local gentry and since the C of E is such a broad church liturgically and theologically it was not usually difficult for them to get a vicar whose outlook fitted their own. In the 17th and 18th centuries this leaves the class of independent small farmers, tradespeople and artisans – the blacksmith, shoemaker, tailor – people who were not poor enough to be forced but not rich enough to change anything. It is they who made up 99% of the Three Denominations (as they called themselves) – Baptists, Presbyterians and Independents (also called Congregationalists) – the Quakers and later the Methodists.

By the 19th century the English Presbyterians had died out or become Unitarians (all recent Presbyterian churches are Scottish imports, itself a fact which may be significant for your ancestry). Quaker numbers exploded dramatically in the 1650s but declined equally dramatically in the 1740s and 1750s and by the 19th century they were a small and very separatist group; nonconformist life was then dominated by Baptists and Methodists, both of which had splintered into a number of churches with separate names.

Generally speaking, Methodists were better-class than Baptists, reflecting the better education of the Methodist ministers who had come out of the Anglican church rather than the more homespun uneducated Baptist ministers. In the villages and in southern England nonconformists remained fairly few in number, but they flourished in the north where large old parishes and the new industrial towns meant that the Anglicans could not keep a tight hold. In towns, the nonconformists dominated; they were the very social group which most prospered from the industrial revolution, and joining with evangelical (ie middle class) Anglicans were able to take control away from the upper class Anglicans: indeed in the north, that class was so small that it was hardly able to put up any fight. It is still true that upper class and lower class people are largely unreflecting C of E while all the religious ferment (even if now directed at moral rather than religious issues) is found among the middle classes who provide us with journalists, teachers and social workers.

To sum up, nonconformist ancestry is found all over the country but only within one narrow social band.

Catholics do not come within this pattern. The laws against them were so severe that they could only survive at all if they were dedicated enough and rich enough. In southern England from the late 1500s to the 1840s Catholicism was chiefly an upper class religion but where there was a gentry family still hanging on to the old religion you would expect to find a high proportion of Catholic tenantry and labourers.

In the Midlands and in the North, especially in Lancashire, Catholics held on in much greater numbers; in the Fylde (the area between Preston and the sea) about 30% of the population was Catholic throughout the 17th and 18th centuries. In Durham, Northumberland, North Yorkshire and parts of the Midlands the figure varies between 5% and 10%. It reaches its lowest point about 1760, not (as so many people imagine) in 1534 when Henry VIII broke the link with Rome.

In the 1840s there were enormous numbers of converts not only from the high-church Anglican upper class but amongst the unchurched working class as well. In fact all the non-conformists gained converts in the 1840s when there was a large class of respectable working class in the towns moving up in the world and willing to go to church if anyone asked it. The Anglicans were not well organised to preach amongst them and Catholics, Baptists, Methodists and Mormons all reaped the benefit. (You don't notice the Mormon converts so much because they encouraged emigration so that no large, long-term communities grew up in England.) Catholic numbers were also swelled by the vast Irish immigration of the 1840s.

The nonconformist churches all grew steadily as those who disagreed with Anglicanism were able to take an effective stand; thus, the further you go back the less likely you are to find nonconformist ancestry or records (except in the case of Quakers 1650–1740 or Huguenots 1680–1760). However, if you go back to the mid-1500s everyone is Catholic; from 1560 to 1760 the numbers steadily declined so that the further you go back the more likely you are to find Catholic ancestry.

All this history is in fact a short cut. Whether in travel, occupation or religion your ancestors are much more likely to have done one thing rather than another (see my remarks at the beginning of this booklet). So much in our ancestors' lives depends on class, an aspect which we like to discount and which those researching from America or Australia are almost bound to misunderstand. All FHS secretaries have seen letters which tell the old family story about the first immigrant to America but which are quite impossible on grounds of class. An 18th century lord's daughter would no more marry a coachman than an orang-utang and if either of them went to America they would be Episcopalians in a city: it is almost inconceivable that their grandchildren would be dirt-farming in the middle-west and going to revivals. An awful lot of people seem to think that if Grandma was a great lady then her father must have been a great Lord. One of the reasons why Methodism had so little effect among good-class people (and it was the only non-conformist sect which had any chance) was that they considered it an impertinence to imply that God did not observe the social distinctions but would ignore the deference due to pedigree.

The SoG has published an excellent series of booklets on the records which pertain to various types of nonconformist ancestry in the *My Ancestors Were* . . . series. Two volumes of the *National Index of Parish Registers* relate to nonconformist and Catholic entries and the details of the nonconformist registers at the PRO are included in the county volumes. Full details of Catholic registers will be found in Catholic Missions and Registers in England, Wales and Scotland 1700 – 1880: M. J. Gandy (6 area volumes: 1993).

SUMMARY: Anglican registers are now mostly in CROs and most early nonconformist registers are in the PRO. A high proportion of both are indexed onto the Mormon IGI. Religion was often a matter of class. The upper classes and the working classes were mostly Anglican while most nonconformists were middle class. Catholics might be any class but were concentrated in certain areas.

The Mormon IGI

The International Genealogical Index includes baptisms and marriages from all over the world arranged (as regards the UK) by counties. It is probably the best and most widely used short cut of all. It is now a first port of call for almost any entry and this is absolutely right. On the other hand it has a hypnotic effect on some people who see entries which are right by date and pay no attention to the geography or the denomination. Having drawn up a likely tree on the basis of the IGI they may not hurry to check the original entries or, if they do, may be inclined to discount circumstantial evidence that the entries are not right. None of the following points is new and the Mormons themselves endlessly issue the same warnings:

– The IGI has all the limitations of the original material and the usual crop of transcription errors.

– It isn't complete for the registers of any county and the registers themselves cannot be a complete record of the births and regular unions that there were.

– It is an index and omits all sorts of details which show that an entry which *might* be the one you want isn't.

USE IT. CHECK IT. PROVE IT!

The second point (about completeness) is very important. We have to work with the records we can find. In some cases these have not survived, in many others they were poorly kept or don't give information that we want because they weren't compiled with our purposes in mind. In many cases our ancestors are not there simply because they weren't baptised or married (all our ancestors died, so you can always hope for a record even when, as in Scotland, there is not much likelihood).

In the case of baptism this is most obvious. In the country the vicar and churchwardens could police the labourers and if a child was not brought to baptism they could exert some pressure, but in the towns this was not possible and not attempted. No one knew what children were being born. Vicars had no idea who was in their parish and they simply baptised any children brought to them, then the clerk wrote in the register the details left by any parents who stayed behind afterwards. The urban working class hardly ever went to church after about 1700 though there was a strong superstition in favour of baptism. The point is that parents had complete freedom of choice in this matter: they minded or they didn't, they remembered or they forgot, they had a job-lot done at some point when it seemed to matter or they turned up whenever it suited them at the vicar's advertised time ('Infants will be baptised any Sunday at 4.30'). Middle and upper class people were concerned about the baptism certificate as evidence of Anglican status but the working class had no such extra motive and might think it a clever trick to nip out quickly after baptism but before registration – and fee paying.

Marriage is a slightly more complicated question. Our distant ancestors felt themselves bound by engagement (betrothal) and the wedding did not add much to that. A great many of the brides were pregnant when they went to church and there was no shame attached to this provided they were engaged; a fair number of couples even took their first child to the wedding with them and had it baptised on the same day. I have wondered whether it was actually the other way round and that as they were going to church for a baptism they thought they might as well get married. However, sooner or later a great many of our ancestors married. That said, a great many of our ancestors divorced as well. There was no formal means of doing this under church law but in practice plenty of couples parted and each partner was likely to settle down with somebody else. There seem to have been folk methods for validating this, such as saying the betrothal words backwards in front of witnesses at the market cross or some similar public place. The much quoted wife-sales seem to have come under this heading. Where a woman had already gone to live with another man the three of them would meet together to shake hands in public for everyone to see that the first husband let her go voluntarily and the second husband took her on properly. The whole ceremony made clear that everything was above-board and it confirmed the woman's new status and respectability.

The consequence of this is that a great many people not tied by middle class morality spent many years in regular, recognised unions which could not and did not have to have a wedding certificate to back them up. The general 19th century cockney view seems to have been that one wedding does for all: a woman was a married woman once she had been married to anyone regardless of whether she was actually married to her present husband. We still feel that it's a cheek for a single woman to put on a wedding ring but there is no reason why a

divorced woman should take hers off. As long as their first partners were alive neither of the couple was free to marry but if they survived long enough and thought it worth the bother they might do so in old age. These customs were more common in the towns or the wilder places than in settled villages but I do not think anyone has yet produced detailed evidence as to what percentage of our ancestors' marriages took place after their children were born rather than before.
SUMMARY: The Mormon IGI is a marvellous index but is not complete and must always be checked. Many couples were never married and many children were never baptised so even a complete index of the surviving records would not contain some of the material we would like to find.

Has it been done before?

Some readers may imagine that a section such as this should have come earlier. If we are back to parish registers then we have probably reached at least 1800. What a pity if we waste all that effort only to find that someone else has done the research before us.

Well, yes and no. If the first relative you asked had simply got the family tree out of a drawer you would have had a quarter of an hour's enjoyment out of looking at it. Family history is like a crossword puzzle or a jigsaw puzzle – the whole point is the pleasure of doing it. We don't need a family tree like the Germans did to prove that they weren't Jewish, it doesn't make any difference to anyone else whether you can trace back to 1700 or 1500 and if you have taken up this research because you think there's £100,000 in Chancery or that you're the rightful Queen of England then you're barmy. Probate searchers and adoptive children looking for their natural parents are a different kettle of fish but their work is rarely pre-1900. The point of this hobby is the fun, challenge and stimulation of doing it and the endless excuses it offers for wandering along the by-ways of history.

That said, a great deal of work has already been done before and, more important in practice, a great deal of valuable work is being done now. How can you check up on it?

The prime modern sources for the old families of the aristocracy and the landed gentry are *Burke's Peerage*, *Debrett's Peerage* and *Burke's Landed Gentry*. Most good reference libraries have at least one edition and many of the better ones have a number. The pedigrees may go back to before the family received its peerage or settled on the lands with which it is chiefly associated but do remember that the early generations are likely to be unreliable at best and fabricated at worst. Modern editions are likely to be more reliable than older ones as they are to some extent the fruits of scholarship rather than kow-towing to pretensions. After Burke's and Debrett's, check G.W. Marshall's *The Genealogists Guide* (4th edition, 1903, reprinted 1967) and J.B. Whitmore's *A Genealogical Guide* (1953, a continuation of the pedigree lists in Marshall's guide). Each of these indexes an enormous number of trees which had appeared in print. They combed the old genealogical periodicals, the county *Notes and Queries*, the classic county histories etc and are a very reliable guide to what had been published, though not of course any guarantee of its accuracy. T.R. Thomson's *A Catalogue of British Family Histories* (1980) attempted a further up-date.

After the above you should check the document collection and the family history shelves at SoG. Members have been handing in notes and family trees more or less since the Society began in 1911. Many professionals too have deposited their case notes or interesting or systematic extracts of material. You never know what you are going to find. Someone may have saved you hours of work at an inaccessible record office or provided just the one piece of information which conclusively proves (or disproves) the link you have been working on for years.

However, two warnings are necessary. The first is that old material is not trustworthy because it is old. Someone working in the 1920s had fewer and worse facilities than you in researching the 1700s and absolutely no advantages unless perhaps his Latin was better. When the great antiquarians were working in the 19th century they were opening up virgin territory; they gathered what they could, made the best notes they could in the time they had on material which was completely private and to which nobody might have access again. They asked all sorts of local worthies what they knew and wrote it down in case it was valuable. In many cases it wasn't. They were unable to work systematically, they had no rights of access to the material, they had no catalogues or indexes and they had not developed a methodology for organising their results. Every science has to start somewhere and they did marvellous ground-breaking work but what we do is better (if we do it properly) and we must not take on trust anything researched by previous generations let alone accept any traditions which have merely been handed down without proving them for ourselves. I don't mean we mustn't find out what they thought. I don't mean that you mustn't note what the opinion of this or that antiquary was. I mean that in many cases they had no more idea than you have and much less possibility of finding out. Check it out because they suggest it but put it on the tree because *you* have proved it.

The second point is that all the old work is about gentry. Most of our families have risen socially in the last few generations and even if you have not, then the social barriers between yourself and the classes above you have been lowered. If you are a teacher, secretary or computer programmer today then you can have easy access to records through a County Record Office; a teacher, clerk or mechanic a hundred years ago was nowhere near the social level of a vicar and would certainly not have been allowed to look at the records on his own. Genealogy used to be an interesting study for local gentlefolk who probably knew their own ancestry but were interested in documenting connections between the old families of the area or in putting a little history to the monuments in the church. Jane Marple (from Agatha Christie) would have been keen on genealogy if she could have spared the time from solving murders. The oldest publications are always about gentry; later we get a class of family history written by retired professionals or managing directors of long-established family businesses. From big farmers and rich shopkeepers down, nobody before 1950 was writing family histories about ordinary people nor were such people writing about themselves. Ordinary in this context means almost everybody. Thus the references to our surnames in these older books are not going to turn out to be ancestors of most of us. Their descendants are still gentry, know they are descended from them, probably bought the book at the time and still have it somewhere.

One of the first lectures I went to at a newly founded family history society was by the chairman, showing how to organise your research notes and using his own family as an example. His tree went back to the 1300s in the male line, 'but I've just got to prove this link'. This link was that a farmer in the 1680s was the grandson of a spare uncle on the tree which some gentleman had recorded at a Herald's Visitation in the 1660s. Despite his pretty chart his tree was ***not*** his tree from the 1680s back. A great many people think they know the early generations of their family because they are in print and that the only problem they have is linking the bottom of an upper class tree with the top of their middle or working class one, excusing the whole fiction on the basis that it must be through younger sons who didn't inherit or because elder sons were cut off with a shilling for marrying beneath them. If you like that sort of thing give up genealogy and write historical romances.

The work you need has been done in the last generation by people exactly like yourself but sufficiently distant in cousinship for you not to have heard of them. They are also members of the FHS and have published their interests in

- the FHS *Members' Interests*
- *The National Genealogical Directory*
- *The Genealogical Research Directory*
- the *British Isles Genealogical Register*
- the advertisement sections of any FHS magazine, *The Genealogists Magazine* (SoG), *Family Tree Magazine* or any similar publication
- the Guild of One Name Studies.

In this connection colonial cousins are vital. It is tempting for people in the UK to imagine that Australians and Americans need our records but we don't need theirs unless we take an interest in distant descendants. However, this is not true. The fact that so many Americans have taken so much interest in the early colonial settlers in New England and Virginia in particular means that work on our 17th century records was being carried out by them some generations before family history became popular over here and a lot of excellent research has been published in America. Now that microfilm and microfiche copies are so widely available researchers abroad can work on exactly the same material as we can and are at no disadvantage if they do their homework. Branches of your family which emigrated may have taken the old Family Bible with them or may have letters giving news of the old people in England when all you have is news of the young people in Australia (fascinating of course but no help in tracing backwards). Even the records may help. The death certificates of some Australian States give information on parents or marriage for which there is no equivalent in the UK, while immigrants to America usually took out naturalisation papers which record place of origin. If your mysterious London grandfather's brother was from Aberdeen then the chances are he was too. If you find that someone is advertising research on a family in which you are interested always write and offer to be helpful. They may know more than you – or they may know very little now but research the line more actively than you in the future and be very happy to share their great deal of work with you because you wrote a friendly letter making a few suggestions and regretting you could not help. And of course advertise your own lines of research as well.

In recent years there has been some growth of the idea of publishing details of what you know rather than what you want to know. *The Family History Knowledge Book* is fairly widely available but there is a lot of room for development in this aspect of family history publicity.

SUMMARY: Check published or deposited material but always go back to the original sources and prove the tree for yourself. Contact distant cousins who are working on the ancestry now (another reason why you must join the relevant FHS).

Heraldry

This extremely interesting subject simply represents a pitfall for most family historians. It is certainly closely allied to upper class genealogy (I leave out coats of arms of cities, livery companies and life peers etc). *If* your ancestors were of that class then they may well have had a coat of arms and you should certainly read the SoG leaflet *The Right To Arms*. If they were not upper class they did not have a coat of arms and any that you come across with the same surname as you don't relate to you. A coat of arms is not attached to a surname. It is borne by the male descendants of the man to whom it was granted and the right does not pass through women. There are many instances where heraldic heiresses have transmitted their fathers' Arms through quarters but this is only possible when the husband has a coat of arms of his own already.

A coat of arms has always been a matter of prestige. However much your ancestors may have sunk in the social scale, until they got as low as you, if they had a coat of arms they would not conceivably have forgotten it. This includes if they went to America or Australia. If you were entitled to a coat of arms you would always have known and used it; if this is the first time you have really thought about it then it doesn't apply to you. Even if you have always used it, it may not apply to you. People have been copying the family coats of arms out of Peerage books ever since they were published on the basis that if it's the same name it must be ours – anyway, everyone's related if you go back far enough. Grandpa too may have bought a plaque through a newspaper advertisement or off a stall. The coat of arms on Uncle Jack's spoons may mean he won a rifle competition, bought A Present From Bognor or stole them from British Railways. Similarly Hotel Splendide on Auntie's towels is not the name of the ancestral mansion.

My rule of thumb is this. Would your grandmother have gone to tea with Jane Marple; would your great-great-grandmother have been welcome in a Jane Austen drawing room. If not then *forget heraldry: it ain't for the likes of us, dearie*.

SUMMARY: Most people don't have a coat of arms. If you have not heard of one up to now then you haven't got one.

ORGANISING THE MATERIAL

If the records were good and your family were Anglican and stayed in the same place then a straightforward tree could be compiled from family knowledge, GRO, census and parish registers. All the other categories of records either put flesh on the bones, help you solve problems or confirm the theories you built on the basic sources. By the time you have traced back to 1800 you will have got involved in such an infinite number of possibilities that no specific advice of mine is going to apply to you. You will be the world expert on your family, on certain records, areas, occupations, chapels; you will have pushed back the frontiers of ignorance a little further, contributed something to the sum of human knowledge, paid tribute to the memory of the sturdy, hardworking, decent folk who sired you and handed down to posterity a crafted heirloom which future generations will cherish. Or you will have cobbled together a garbled mish-mash of half-truths and mistakes and launched it on an indifferent younger generation to lurk in a drawer and do harm years after you have gone.

Many of the errors with which too many family trees are larded have crept in because the research material was not well organised. Not everyone is good at carrying names, dates and relationships in their head and some of the people who think they are make the worst mistakes. I once read a long explanation justifying the decision that one baptism in 1825 was right rather than another in the same year when the whole point of the exercise was to check the birth of a man who said he was 25 in 1861 (so they should have been looking about 1835). I have already referred to doing your homework on what a record office has got before you go, what you want to do when you get there and what you are going to do about it afterwards. Of course the second and third stages cannot be too structured as you don't know exactly what you are going to find.

Above all, work out in advance what material you want to work on or what problems you want to solve and how. Write yourself simple instructions, check they are right while you are still at home and believe them when you get to the repository. Thinking on your feet is always risky, especially when you come across entries which might be connected. (Could this George be one of mine? Is 1815 the right sort of date for the marriage of George and Ann? Didn't Thomas have a son George or was that on one of my other lines? Do we know what happened to Edward? If this Mary Ann who died in 1823 aged 40 is actually Mary the wife of James then the one who died in 1806 with no age given must be either the baby baptised in 1805 or the very old widow of Samuel because the one who died in 1838 aged 80 must be the wife of John who died in 1842 and should have been 84 though the register says 88. Or have I got that wrong?)

Clearly you need your notes but here comes warning number two: don't take too much with you. You need what you need but you don't need everything you've got. Rolls of wallpaper are out, so is anything over A4 size. If you use Filofax or Genfile systems, these are fine. Take your working tree and the notes and material which relate to what you are going to work on but even then try to take the minimum. You don't, for example, need the evidence (such as GRO certificates) on which you based your proved tree. You aren't going to have to demonstrate the truth of your theories to anyone else and as long as you were confident about it at home then you don't need to question it while you're working.

As you go through the records always make a clear note of everything you have searched with covering dates. This can seem like a waste of time as you think you won't forget, but you will and it is more of a waste of time to rack your brains or comb the shelves trying to find a reference you think you saw but want to check. Always make a note of anything you want to do but didn't have time for, or a bright idea that flitted through your head while you were too busy to follow it up. Above all note down gaps in the records. You haven't searched baptisms 1680 – 1720 if the vicar clearly gave up registering anyone for five years in the middle; you haven't searched all the parishes round Canterbury if two of the registers haven't survived and one is unfit for production.

Keep your references in loose leaf binders and write references to separate names on separate sheets so that you can file the notes alphabetically with simplicity. If you are descended from a number of families in the same area then you are likely to take every entry of all those names out of any register you search. If you take them all on the same piece of paper you will have to recopy them. Why make life hard for yourself? Here the computer/word processor people will feel smug but high tech is itself an enormous time waster. Computers are marvellous for some jobs but quite unnecessary for others, like using a food processor when a wooden spoon would be fine. Still, for quite a lot of people genealogy is only an excuse for playing with their computer and they're entitled to their fun.

SUMMARY: Keep it clear. Keep it simple. Do your homework carefully.

FAMILY HISTORY SOCIETIES

I keep mentioning these and referring you to them. The addresses of the secretaries are all listed in the Appendix and on the back of the FFHS *Family History News and Digest* and you must join every one which covers an area where you are tracing ancestors as well as joining the one in the area where you live. This is not negotiable. From your own area you will get access to a bookstall, good advice, like-minded friends, outings and projects, regular lectures and up-to-date news of what is going on in our very busy world. You can also learn about the history of your area and get a better view of how things were in your ancestor's area from knowing how they were in yours.

By joining FHSs elsewhere you get, above all, local knowledge. People who live in an area know things automatically which no outsider could guess. Read the articles, advertise your family interests, swap work with people there who will do things for you if you will do things for them, tell them what you know in case it is helpful to somebody else but above all use them to keep in touch with what is going on in the area. The chief vehicle is the magazine: it should have the programme of meetings (which you won't usually be going to), news of projects, articles about the families and places and special records of the area but above all notices and reviews of what is available in the area which you wouldn't hear about if you live elsewhere: what is in the local museum, what special indexes are in the Local Studies Library, who is the local expert and what are the classic histories of the local parishes, mansions, almshouses, hospitals, which church has just published its centenary history, who was using the local paper to advertise for old relatives, where can you get copies of photographs of the area? It has to be said that some FHS magazines don't have enough of this sort of material; some editors do not seem to have a policy but just publish whatever comes to hand, but as a Londoner with lots of non-London ancestry, when I join an area society I want to know about the area. Editors and secretaries please note: members are entitled to ask you questions. If they keep asking the same questions then it's a sign that your magazine needs an article on that subject.

Membership of an FHS is your best short cut to a hundred pieces of knowledge about the area, all of which are interesting and some of which may be essential to drawing up your tree and picturing the family correctly.

That said, remember that the majority of FHS secretaries, editors and co-ordinators are volunteers and that they do the work for love. An annual subscription of between £8 and £12 does not entitle you to pester them endlessly and you are certainly not entitled to ask them to carry out research for you except in those indexes or transcripts which the society offers to search for its members. Do your own homework and if you cannot do your own research then either set up an exchange arrangement or contact a professional. You will often find that local members of the society will go to a lot of extra trouble for you in return for an extra donation to the funds. As always a sense of proportion is everything: some people write, 'Please do this quickly as it is very important to me' and I find this an immediate turn-off. This is only a hobby after all; your ancestors are stone-dead and don't care whether you're tracing them or not; another few weeks won't hurt.

I said above that joining the relevant FHS was not negotiable. Some people will object that they have ancestors in a dozen different counties and that joining all those societies will be expensive. Perhaps, but it's still not negotiable. If you haven't got a brush you can't paint the wall and it's no good trying to do it with the hammer you bought last week. If your pocket won't stretch then decide which ancestors you want to trace now and leave the others till later. You don't have to trace them at all but if you do, do it properly.

Remember my remarks on accuracy and proof?

SUMMARY: Join the FHS in your home area and any areas where you are tracing your ancestors.

SHORT CUTS TO AVOID

You will have gathered by now that my idea of a short cut is not necessarily one which is quicker; it is also one which helps accuracy and reliability. Working quickly is a short cut to error and if you have got the wrong certificate for your grandfather's birth then all the previous generations are someone else's ancestry and you've got to start again. So I am going to end by listing a number of things you must *not* do:

(a) *Don't make assumptions without testing them.* See my previous remarks about the wife in the census not being the mother of the children. A tree I worked on in my early years went wrong because we had been told the year a man retired (in 1960) and had assumed he was 65.

(b) *Don't lead your relatives*. If you tell them the answer they may agree with you or they may go on talking about something else leading you to suppose they agreed with you. It is difficult to keep the balance between prompting them and pre-empting the answer, between getting the answers to specific questions you have and letting them tell you what they think is interesting or important.

(c) *Never take a short cut without being aware of it*. If you think you can start with your grandparents' birth certificates then you have decided not to buy their marriage certificate. This would have stated the names of their fathers. If the birth certificates you choose to buy are wrong you won't know because you haven't got the marriage certificate to check against. This may be fine, but you need to be aware of it.

(d) *Don't forget the difference between positive evidence and negative evidence*. Positive evidence is where the information you wanted is found or you got a firm reliable statement that such-and-such was true. Negative evidence is when you have eliminated all the possibilities and only one is left. Sherlock Holmes said this last possibility, however unlikely, must be true but he assumed you really had got all the possible options. In family history this is difficult to know. Even if you have searched every record available there may still be other possibilities not in the records. When you have just one candidate left he may still be wrong!

(e) *Don't trust lists*. The fact that a name appears in this place at this time is not evidence that he fits on your tree. He may be an outsider who lived in the area for a very short time; he may be a cousin you haven't heard of yet; the authorities may be

214 WOODBRIDGE DIRECTORY.

MASTER MARINERS.
*Those marked * are Shipowners.*
Adams Edward, Common quay
Allen Thomas, Castle street
*Amos Wm. and Jas. Castle street
Bardwell G. S. Brook street
Braham Robert, Sun street
Bridges Wm. Brook street
Brightwell John, New street
Broomby John W. Cumberland st
Dorrell Wm. Theatre street
*Dowsing James, Thoroughfare
Elmore Samuel, Castle street
Fisk John, Theatre street
Garrard Charles, Quay lane
Hart Edmund, Brook street
How John, Common quay
Hunt George, Quay lane
Keeble John, Castle street
Knights Robert, Deben street
*Levett Wm. Castle street
Marsh John, Quay lane
Marsh Wm. Quay lane
*Moor John, New street
Newson David, Brewers' lane
Nunn John, Brook street
Passiful Edward, Brook street
Read Edward Bond, and Baldry, Common Quay
Revans John, Brook street
*Row George, Cumberland street
Skipper S. Angel street
Smith Thomas, Castle street
Smith Wm. Cumberland street
Woodroffe Wm. Seckford street
*Trott George, Castle street
*Trott Wm. Chapel lane
Woods Robert, Bredfield street

MILLINERS, &c.
Cullum and Ling, Thoroughfare
Fuller Louisa, Seckford street
Gibbs Harriet, Seckford street
Haswell Caroline, Thoroughfare
Kemp Susan, Market place
Nading M. A. Thoroughfare
Olding Harriet, Thoroughfare
Simpson Ann, New street
Stanford & Freeman, Thoroughfare
Waspe Mary Ann, Quay lane
Ward Susan, Thoroughfare

PAINTERS, PLUMBERS, & GLAZIERS.
Allen Loder, Church street
Cooke Wm. and Hy. Thoroughfare
Heffer John, Seckford street
Kell James and Charles, Thoroughfr
Mallett John, New street
Mallett Wm. Market place
Moore Wm. Christopher, New st

ROPE & TWINE MAKERS.
Cork Henry, Church street
Giles John, New street

SADDLERS & HARNESS MKS.
Birch Robert, New street
Durrant Isaac, Thoroughfare
Kirby Robert, Market place

SAIL MAKERS.
Horn Wm. Bell, Common quay
Nichols John, Common quay

SHIP & BOAT BUILDERS.
Garrard Wm. (boat) Brook street
Taylor Wm. Limekiln quay Ship-yard & Patent Slip; h Thorofare

SHIP OWNERS.
(See Master Mariners, &c.)

SHOPKEEPERS.
Bird Robert, Castle street
Breckles Margt. Castle street
Clark Eliza, Theatre street
Coleman Husting, Seckford street
Cullham Samuel, Cumberland street
Easter Abraham, Castle street
Garrard Wm. Brook street
Glanfield Wm. Bredfield street
Hartridge Wm. horse letter & omnibus owner, New street
Hawkins Joseph, Thoroughfare
Keeble Ann, Castle street
Lambert Mary, Cumberland street
Pizey Philip, New street
Roberts Thos. S. Theatre street
Sawyer Christian, Chapel lane
Smith Elizabeth, Seckford street
Stephenson Robert, Seckford street
Turner Samuel, Bredfield street
Woods Robert, Bredfield street

STAY MAKERS.
Field Sophia, Seckford street
Leverett Caroline, Cumberland st
Quinton Elizabeth, Market place

STONE & MARBLE MASON.
Smyth James, Thoroughfare

STRAW HAT MAKERS.
Broadbank Hephzibah, Thoroughfare
Cullingford Hannah, Thoroughfare
Moore Eliza, New street
Moss Hannah, Seckford street
Pite Mary Ann, Church street
Wade George, Cumberland street
Wright Elizabeth, Brook street

SURGEONS.
Gissing Samuel, Market place
Jones Richard, Church street
Lynn Geo. D. (physician) Church st

WOODBRIDGE DIRECTORY. 215

Marshall Charles, Castle street
Moore Nathl. & Son, Church street
Welton (Wm.) and Bligh (Richd.) Thoroughfare and Cumberland st

SURVEYORS, *(Land, &c.)*
Lankester J. *(river,)* Cumberland st
Lockwood Alfd. (architect,) Castle st
Moulton Benj. Thoroughfare
Pattisson W. (& architect,) Brook st
Thompson Geo. (county surveyor,) Thoroughfare

TAILORS & DRAPERS.
Brown James, Thoroughfare
Bodgener Henry, New street
Chappell Wm. Geo. Church street
Christopher Wm. Cumberland st
Freeman Charles, Thoroughfare
Gall John, Castle street
Hunt John, Church street
Lyons Robert, Theatre street
Mallett Jonathan, Market place
Moss James, Cumberland street
Simpson Wm. New street
Whistock Wm. Thoroughfare
Wright (Jeremiah) & Stock (Saml.) Church street

TALLOW CHANDLERS.
Gross & Thompson, Thoroughfare
Stanford Henry, Market place

TANNER.
Bond John, Brewer's ln; h *Ipswich*

TIMBER MERCHANTS.
Colchester Wm. and Co. (& slate,) Common quay
Grimwood Thomas, Thoroughfare

TOY DLRS. *(See Hardware.)*

UMBRELLA MKRS.
Pooley Samuel, Bredfield street
Revett Brady, (cutler,) New street

WATCH & CLOCK MAKERS.
Baker James, Brook street
Fisher John Forsdick, Market place
Gant Robert Drake, Thoroughfare
Hildyards John, Thoroughfare
Taylor John, New street

WHEELWRIGHTS.
Calver Chas. Brett & Ts. Theatre st
Quadling Geo. Bredfield street

WHITESMITHS.
Baxter Wm. Brook street
Dowsing James, Chapel lane
Fisher Richard, Common quay
Owles Charles, New street
Smyth Henry, Seckford street
Stananought John, New street

WINE & SPIRIT MERTS.
Brook Abm. & Son, Church street
Edwards Henry, (and ship owner,) Thoroughfare and Brook street
Gross and Thompson, Thoroughfare
Wincopp Wm. Market place

COACHES.
Mail, to London, at ½ past 10 night, and to Yarmouth, at ½ past 4 morning, from the Post-office
Shannon, to London, ¼ past 10 mng. and to Halesworth, ½ past 4 aft; and the *Retaliator*, to London, 20 min. before 8 morning, from the Crown; *Original Blue*, to London, ¾ past 12 at noon; and to Saxmundham and Yarmouth, ½ past 2 afternoon, from the Sun
Mail Cart, to Orford, &c. 6 morng. from the Royal Oak

OMNIBUSES
To meet the *London Steamers* at *Ipswich*, every Mon. and Thurs. from the King's Arms; and every Tues. and Friday, from the Cross, at ½ past 6 morning: return following days to Saxmundham, Framlingham, Wickham-Market, &c. Oxborrow's Omnibus, from the Sun, to *Ipswich*, daily, during summer; and Smith's, from the Royal Oak, to *Aldeburgh*, Tues. Thursday and Saturday

CARRIERS.
Marked 1, stop at the Anchor; 2, Boat; 3, King's Arms; 4, Red Lion; 5, Royal Oak; 6, Sun; 7, Wellington; 8, White Horse; and 9, at the Crown inn

Places. *Carriers.*
London, &c. H. R. & J. Smith, Sat. Tue. & Thu. from the Thghfare
5 Alderton, A. Hill, M. W. Th. & S
3 Bawdsey, P. Cutting, M. W. & F
Bedfield, Smith, (Wagn. & Horses,) Friday
5 Boyton, F. Ashkettle, W. S; 3 P. Cutting, M. W. F; and Cooper, Arnold, and Flory, M. Tues. W. Friday and Saturday
1 Brandeston, Pratt, M. W. and Fri
1 Dallinghoo, J. Sheppard, W. Sat
1 Easton and Earl Soham. C. Pratt, Monday, Wednesday, and Friday
5 Framlingham, S. Exworth, Mon. Thursday; and 7 *mail cart* daily
2 Framsden, Flick, Tuesday
5 Fressingfield, A. Hart, Wednesday

Don't trust lists! Seeing something in print does not make it true. Even those useful directories are out of date before they are printed, and firms often trade under the founder's name long after he has died.

using an out-of-date list. Directories are always up to a year out of date, shops and firms often trade under the name of the founder long after he has died and widows who stay on in the same house often don't bother to alter their listing in the directory, so that the man whose initial appears in the book may have died 10, 20 or 30 years before.

(f) *Don't think you have all the facts*. In the country and with local names it is often possible to feel that you have checked all the sources, got all the entries and that everything must fit together somehow. In towns there is never this certainty, always the possibility of wild cards turning up, the awareness that half the entries you need aren't there and half the entries you have got belong on some other tree.

(g) *Don't rely on a family tradition*. There is often a grain of truth in them but stories can easily get attached to the wrong person (when we tell a story about Grandma do we mean my Grandma or your Grandma my mother). They get exaggerated by imagination (rich Uncle George was the only one in the family to have his own watch and chain). This is very much the case with money your family didn't inherit; thousands of pounds now in Chancery may have started off as £20 – well worth a family quarrel in 1905 but not a fortune even then.

(h) *Don't insist on certain spelling forms*. Say the name out loud in the accent of the area, then pretend you're an old gaffer with no teeth. Now be a deaf, indifferent clerk who doesn't come from the area and thinks he hasn't got time to waste on yokels. His pen scratches and blots and he's got the beginnings of arthritis or palsy. Then let the ink fade for 200 years and get the register transcribed by a beginner, typed up by someone who was watching the television and spot-checked by someone who thought it was probably all right so why bother. A computer with a blip prints it out and Bob's Your Uncle – lost for ever!

(i) *Don't leave sources part searched without a clear note*, repeated whenever you copy the results.

(j) *Don't stop at the first likely entry*. Even the rarest name can occur a number of times in the same family. The first one you come across may be a cousin of the one you want. He may even be an elder brother who died and they gave the next child the same name. If one was born in January 1812 and the other born in December 1812 you might say it doesn't matter much but it does. If we're going to trace our ancestry let's get it right.

(k) *Don't use indexes without checking the beginning of the index, the title page and the foreword*. I have covered this at length elsewhere.

(l) Last of all, *don't think it a waste of time to do something again*. If you go through a register a second time you may find the entries you missed the first time, you may realise that some odd spelling actually refers to a missing ancestor of yours or you may pick up references to people you didn't know were related the first time you checked that source, eg the descendants of married sisters whose marriages you hadn't yet found.

GETTING THE SOURCES TO COME TO YOU

Over the past 30 years, a great deal of material has been gathered in County Record Offices and Local Studies Libraries so that you can now see a wide range of sources in one place. Increasingly, also, copies of material have become available for use away from the original. Some of this may be available at centres which are more convenient to you; a great deal may also be worked on at home, though here again you may have to consult your purse.

Any of the following possibilities may be right for your circumstances.

(a) *The Society of Genealogists*. This is, without question, the finest genealogical library in the UK. If you can get to London, then you will never exhaust the interest of the material it contains; long after you have given up tracing your ancestors, you will still enjoy simply browsing. Much of the contents is available for loan to members, so if you live too far away to visit or cannot go often you may still be able to have the books you want to see posted home to you. The majority of microfiches and microfilms are available for postal loan and this is a growing proportion of the collection.

If material you want is not yet available at the SoG you may consider sponsoring its purchase. You pay half the cost of the item and then have exclusive use of it (including at home) for the first three months. After that it is generally available in the library which means that in practice you can use it as much as you like. This sponsorship scheme is particularly useful for big series (such as Scottish census) where the SoG has a rolling programme but the particular item you want may not get to the top of the shopping list for a long time.

(b) *Family History Centres*. The Church of Jesus Christ of Latter Day Saints, also known as the Mormons or LDS has centres all over the UK through which you can get access to their international collection of sources. All centres have the IGI, a stock of basic microfilms and reference works and the catalogue of the material held in the main genealogical library in Salt Lake City. Any material in the catalogue can be ordered for a charge so low that it can barely cover the postage. The order takes a few weeks to come through and then you can have exclusive use of the film for a few weeks at the Centre. Since the Mormons have had a worldwide microfilming programme for many years this is not only the easiest and cheapest but often in practice the only way you can get access to certain material.

The staff at the LDS Family History Centres are usually very friendly and their fantastic service is offered free to everyone without any need to be in sympathy with Mormonism. However, the staff are amateur volunteers and may not have any special genealogical knowledge so if you ask questions you may not get very useful answers. You don't expect the girl at the public library to know who did the murders, do you?

(c) *Family History Society collections*. Many FHSs have extensive libraries or are willing to lend transcripts of the material they have worked on or been given. Their magazines often contain letters from members offering to search particular sources. The people who compiled the index or offered the service often enjoy being asked and will go to a lot of trouble on your behalf, perhaps helping in other directions if they draw a blank in the particular source you asked them about. I have already mentioned the possibility that you can offer to look things up in your area in exchange for someone looking up material in their area for you.

A lot of FHS projects have been published and are available for sale. Many record offices have now produced microfilms or microfiches for sale to individuals or to societies and I have already underlined the usefulness of photocopies. It costs money of course, but it's money well spent if you value your time.

(d) *The inter-library loan system*. This still functions well and for a very small charge you can borrow almost any book in print and a fair number of those which are out-of-print. Don't push your luck and ask for the Domesday Book!

SUMMARY: For a complete list of *The Society of Genealogists* publications see Appendix I, page 70.

For a complete list of *Family History Centres* (The Church of Jesus Christ of Latter Day Saints, also known as The Mormons or LDS) see Appendix II, page 90.

For a complete list of *Family History Societies* see Appendix II, page 83.

NOW READ ON

Appendix I

Now it is time to beg, borrow or . . . (No! Certainly not). In the following bibliography you will find lists which are up-to-date at the moment and are offered as a suggestion. Through your local FHS you can keep an eye out for the new material which is appearing all the time and making our hobby steadily easier, more stimulating and more successful.

You'll soon be back to 1066!

Gibson's Guides for Genealogists

Bishops' Transcripts and Marriage Licences (3rd edn.)
Census Returns on Microfilm (6th edn.)
Coroners' Records (reprint)
Electoral Registers Since 1832 (2nd edn.)
Hearth Tax Returns and Other Later Stuart Tax Lists
List of Londoners
Local Census Listings 1522 – 1930
Local Newspapers: 1750 – 1920
Marriage, Census and Other Indexes (5th edn.)
Militia Lists and Musters (1757 – 1876) (3rd edn.)
Poll Books c 1695 – 1872 (3rd edn.)
Probate Jurisdictions (4th edn.)
Quarter Session Records
Record Offices: How to find them (6th edn.)
Tudor and Stuart Muster Rolls

FFHS Publications

Family History News and Digest
An Introduction to Irish Research
Army Records for Family Historians

Basic Sources for Family Historians (3rd edn.)
Beginning Your Family History (5th edn.)
Book of Trades Part 1
Book of Trades Part 2
Current Pubs by Member Societies on Microfiche (3rd edn.)
Current Publications by Member Societies (8th edn.)
Dating Old Photographs
Family Historians Enquire Within (5th edn.) (enlarged and updated)
Family History Record Sheets
Forming A One-Name Group (4th edn.)
Glossary of Household, Farming and Trade Terms (3rd edn.)
How to Record Your Family Tree
How to Tackle Your Family Tree (revised and updated)
In and Around Record Offices (3rd edn.)
Latin Glossary for Family Historians
Manorial Records (How to Locate and Use)
Monumental Inscriptions (4th edn.)
Nonconformity (Understanding the History and Records of)
Records of the RAF
Register of One-Name Studies (9th edn.)
Sources for One-Name Studies
Surname Periodicals
The Scots Overseas (Select Bibliography)
Was Your Grandfather a Railwayman? (2nd edn.)
World War I Army Ancestry (2nd edn.)
Location of British Army Records (3rd edn.)
More Sources of WWI Army Ancestry (2nd edn.)

Raymond Bibliographies and Periodicals

British Genealogical Periodicals, Vol. 1
British Genealogical Periodicals, Vol. 2 Part 1
British Genealogical Periodicals, Vol. 2 Part 2
English Genealogy
Genealogical Bibliography, Dorset
Genealogical Bibliography, Gloucestershire/Bristol
Genealogical Bibliography, Somerset
Genealogical Bibliography, Suffolk
Occupational Sources for Family Historians

Other publications available through FFHS

Ancestor Trail in Ireland
Computers In Family History (4th edn.)
Handbook on Irish Genealogy: How to Trace Your Ancestors in Ireland
Irish Genealogy: A Record Finder
Making Use of the Census
Scottish Roots
Tracing Your Scottish Ancestors
Tracing Your Ancestors in the PRO (54th edn.)

Society of Genealogists publications

Ancestry Chart 32 in x 23 in on stout paper for recording eight generations
Birth Brief Form (A3 size with margin for binding) for recording four generations
Census Indexes in the Library of the Society of Genealogists (2nd edn., 1990, 41 pp.)
Dates and Calendars for the Genealogist, by C. Webb (amended reprint, 1991, 36 pp.)
Directories and Poll Books in the Library of the Society of Genealogists, Editor L.W.L. Edwards
Directory of British Peerages from Earliest Times to the Present Day, Editor F.L. Leeson (1984, 174 pp.)
Examples of Handwriting 1550 – 1650, by W.S.B. Buck (1982, 72pp.)
Family Tree Detective (2nd edn.)
An Index to Bank of England Will Extracts 1807 – 1845 (1991, 310 pp. A4 size in comb binding), also available in microfiche (see below)
An Index to Wills Proved in the Prerogative Court of Canterbury 1750 – 1800, Editor A.J. Camp (10% discount if order placed with the Society)

Vol. 1 A – Bh (1976, 414 pp.)
Vol. 2 Bi – Ce (out of print but available on microfiche, see below)
Vol. 3 Ch – G (1984, out of print but available on microfiche, see below)
Vol. 4 H – M (1988, out of print but available on microfiche, see below)
Vol. 5 N – Sh (1991, 259 pp.)
Vol. 6 Si – Z (1992, 310 pp.)

Lancashire Association Oath Rolls 1696, Editor W. Gandy (1985, 131 pp.)

Leaflets of the Society of Genealogists (advice for beginners)

No. 1 Publications Price List free
No. 2 Genealogy: A Basic Bibliography (4 pp.)
No. 3 Family Records and their Layout (4 pp.)
No. 4 Note Taking and Keeping for Genealogists (4 pp.)
No. 5 Genealogy as a Career (4 pp.)
No. 6 Notes for Americans on Tracing British Ancestry (4 pp.)
No. 7 The Relevance of Surnames (4 pp.)
No. 8 Protestation Returns of 1641 – 42 (4 pp.)
No. 9 Starting Genealogy (4 pp.)
No. 10 Irregular Border Marriages (4 pp.)
No. 11 Genealogical Research in New Zealand (4 pp.)
No. 12 Army Muster and Description Books (4 pp.)
No. 13 Society of Genealogists Floor Guide (4 pp.)
No. 15 The Right to Arms (4 pp.)
No. 17 Essential Addresses (4 pp.)
No. 18 The Data Protection Act and Genealogists (6pp.)
No. 19 Army Research, Selected Bibliography (4 pp.)
No. 20 Navy Research, Selected Bibliography (4 pp.)
No. 21 Has It Been Done Before? (4 pp.)
No. 23 County Codes (4 pp.)
No. 24 In Search of a Soldier Ancestor (4 pp.)
No. 25 Guide to Sources for One-Name Studies in the SoG Library (4 pp.)
No. 26 Sources for Nottinghamshire Genealogists in the SoG Library (4 pp.)
No. 27 Sources for Lancashire Genealogists in the SoG Library
No. 28 Employing a Professional Researcher: A Practical Guide (4 pp.)

A List of Parishes in Boyd's Marriage Index (6th edn., 1987, reprinted 1992, 54 pp.)

London Family History Societies and Registration Districts, map with lists on reverse, 1991

Marriage Licences: Abstracts and Indexes in the Library of the Society of Genealogists, compiled by L. Collins (4th edn., 1991, 26 pp.)

Monumental Inscriptions in the Library of the Society of Genealogists.

Part 1. Southern England, Editor L. Collins (1984, 51pp.)
Part 2. Northern England, Wales, Scotland, Ireland and Overseas, Editors L. Collins and M. Morton (1987, 46 pp.)

Monuments and their Inscriptions, by H.L. White (1976, 64 pp.) (advice on recording gravestones, memorials).

My Ancestor was a Merchant Seaman: How Can I Find Out More About Him?, by C.T. and M.J. Watts (reprinted with addenda 1991, 84 pp.)

My Ancestor was Jewish: How Can I Find Out More About Him? (Currently out of print. A new edition will be available shortly.)

My Ancestor was a Migrant (in England or Wales): How Can I Trace Where He Came From?, by A.J. Camp (1987, 44 pp.)

My Ancestor was in the British Army: How Can I Find Out More About Him?, by C.T. and M.J. Watts (1992, 122 pp.)

My Ancestors Came with the Conqueror – Those Who Did and Some of Those Who Probably Did Not, by A.J. Camp (corrected reprint 1990, 84 pp.)

My Ancestors were Baptists: How Can I Find Out More About Them?, by G.R. Breed (revised 1988, 51 pp.)

My Ancestors were Congregationalists (in England and Wales), by D.J.H. Clifford (with a list of registers), (1992, 93 pp.)

My Ancestors were Manorial Tenants: How Can I Find Out More About Them?, by P.B. Park (1990, 49 pp.)

My Ancestors were Methodists: How Can I Find Out More About Them?, by W. Leary (2nd edn., 1990, 74 pp.)

My Ancestors were Quakers: How Can I Find Out More About Them?, by E.H. Milligan and M.J. Thomas (1983, 37 pp.)

National Index of Parish Registers (the whereabouts of original registers, transcripts, Bishops' Transcripts)
(Vols 1, 2, 5, 11 Pt 1, and 12 are out of print)

- Vol. 3 Sources for Roman Catholic and Jewish Genealogists and Family History (incl. Index to Vols. 1 – 3, 1974, 264 pp.)
- Vol. 4 Part 1 Surrey (1990, 200 pp.)
- Vol. 6 Part 1 Staffordshire (2nd edn., 1992, 100 pp.)
- Vol. 6 Part 2 Nottinghamshire (1988, 87 pp., paperback)
- Vol. 7 East Anglia: Cambridgeshire, Norfolk, Suffolk (1983, 278 pp.)
- Vol. 8 Part 1 Berkshire (1989, 128 pp.)
- Vol. 8 Part 2 Wiltshire (1992, 114 pp.)
- Vol. 9 Part 1 Bedfordshire and Huntingdonshire (1991, 120 pp.)
- Vol. 9 Part 2 Northamptonshire (1991, 86 pp.)
- Vol. 9 Part 3 Buckinghamshire (1992, 82 pp)
- Vol. 13 Parish Registers of Wales (1986, 217 pp.)

Parish Register Copies in The Library of the Society of Genealogists (10th edn., 1992)

Record Cards: Personal (75 per pkt.); Census (50 per pkt.)
School, University and College Registers and Histories in the Library of the Society of Genealogists (1988, 43 pp.)
Sources for Anglo Indian Genealogists in the Library of the Society of Genealogists, by N.C. Taylor (1990, 12 pp.)
Sources for Irish Genealogy in the Library of the Society of Genealogists, compiled by A.J. Camp (1990, 16 pp.)
The Trinity House Petitions: A Calendar of the Records of the Corporation of Trinity House, London in the Library of the Society of Genealogists (1987, 303 pp.)
Using the Library of the Society of Genealogists (1992, 18 pp.)

Society of Genealogists publications on microfiche

1 Bankrupt Directory 1820 – 1843 (8 fiche)
2 Lloyds Captains Register 1869 (14 fiche)
3 Buckinghamshire Poll Book 1784 (incl. MS material) (new improved filming, 3 fiche)
4 Cambridgeshire Poll Book 1722 (2 fiche)
5 Dorset Poll Book 1807 (2 fiche)
6 Nottinghamshire Poll Book 1754 (1 fiche)
7 Sussex Poll Book 1734 (2 fiche)
8 Wiltshire Poll Book 1722 (2 fiche)
9 Leicestershire Poll Book 1741 (4 fiche)
10 Bankrupt Directory 1774 – 1786 (2 fiche)
11 Abstract of 3973 Irish Wills, indexed, compiled by L. Rosbottom (20 fiche)
12 Essex Hearth Tax Assessments 1662, with index (11 fiche)
13 Westminster Poll Book 1749 (5 fiche)
14 Salop Directory 1828 (2 fiche)
15 Staffordshire Directory Part 3 1818 (new improved filming, 3 fiche)
16 Ecclesiastical Directory 1829 (6 fiche)
17 Medical Directory 1847 (6 fiche)
18 Medical Register 1779 (new improved filming, 3 fiche)
19 List of Apothecaries 1815 – 1840 (4 fiche)
20 Law List 1812 (3 fiche)
21 Monumental Inscriptions of Jamaica (7 fiche)
22 Name Index to the 2% Sample of the 1851 Census Returns (and some other transcripts), compiled by Dr. A.M. Stanier (27 fiche)
23 Lockie's Topography of London 1810 (5 fiche)

29 Index to Wills Proved in the PCC 1750 – 1800, Vol. 2 Bi – Ce (8 fiche)
30 Index to Wills Proved in the PCC 1750 – 1800, Vol 3 Ch – G (7 fiche)
31 Index to the Bank of England Will Extracts 1807 – 1845 (6 fiche)

The Society of Genealogists also sells a wide range of other genealogical and related books, including many record office guides, some PRO publications, Family Tree publications, the Genealogical Research Directories, National Genealogical Directories and IHGS parish maps. Send an sae to the Society for its full list.

Selection of PRO information leaflets

No. 37	Access to Public Records
No. 63	Agricultural Statistics: Parish Summaries
No. 13	Air Force: Genealogy, *see also* Pensions
No. 16	Air Force: Operations
No. 50	Air Force: Research and Development
No. 44	Apprenticeships
No. 109	Architectural plans
No. 59	Army: Genealogy
No. 61	Army: Operations 1660 – 1914
No. 6	Army: Operations 1914 – 1919
No. 7	Army: Operations 1939 – 1945
	see also Court Martial, Medals, Militia, Ordnance, Royal Marines
No. 123	Army: Pension Records
No. 26	Assizes
No. 112	Attorneys and Solicitors
	Australia, *see* Convicts
	Births, Marriages and Deaths, *see* Genealogy
	Canals, *see* Transport
No. 10	Census Returns
No. 58	Census Room
No. 62	Census Statistics
	see also Ecclesiastical Census
No. 9	Chancery Lane/Kew: Division of Records
No. 47	Chancery Lane: Are You in the Right Place?
No. 100	Chancery Lane: Document Ordering
No. 52	Chancery Lane: New Readers

USEFUL ADDRESSES

Appendix II

County Record Offices in England & Wales

Several counties now have more than one archive centre, some of which are included below, and it is always recommended that you check on the whereabouts of records *before* making an appointment. For maps and basic information on making use of record offices, the Gibson Guide on *Record Offices: How to find them* is invaluable. London repositories are a maze in themselves: try *London Local Archives* ed. Elizabeth Silverthorne (Guildhall Library and Greater London Archives Network).

AVON: Bath City Record Office, Guildhall, Bath BA1 5AW (01225 477000 ext 7421); Bristol Record Office, B Bond Warehouse, Smeaton Rd, Bristol BS1 6XN (0117 922 5692)
BEDFORDSHIRE: County Hall, Bedford MK42 9AP (01234 228833/ 228777)
BERKSHIRE: Shire Hall, Shinfield Park, Reading RG2 9XD (0118 9233182)
BUCKINGHAMSHIRE: County Hall, Aylesbury HP20 1UA (01296 382587)
CAMBRIDGESHIRE: Shire Hall, Castle Hill, Cambridge CB3 0AP (01223 317281); County Record Office (Huntingdon), Grammar School Walk, Huntingdon PE18 6LF (01480 425842)
CHESHIRE: Duke Street, Chester CH1 1RL (01244 602559); Chester City Records Office, Town Hall, Chester CH1 2HJ (01244 402110)
CLEVELAND: Exchange House, 6 Marton Rd, Middlesborough, Cleveland TS1 1DB (01642 248321)
CORNWALL: County Hall, Truro TR1 3AY (01872 73698)

CUMBRIA: (Carlisle) The Castle, Carlisle CA3 8UR (01228 812416); (Kendal) County Offices, Kendal LA9 4RQ (01539 814330); (Barrow) 140 Duke St, Barrow in Furness LA14 1XW (01229 831269); (Whitehaven) Scotch St, Whitehaven CA28 7BJ

DERBYSHIRE: County Offices, Matlock DE4 3AG (01629 580000)

DEVON: Castle St, Exeter EX4 3PU (01392 384253); North Devon Record Office, North Devon Library, Tuly St, Barnstaple EX31 1EL (01271 388608); West Devon Area Record Office, Unit 3 Clare Place, Coxside, Plymouth PL4 0JW (01752 385940)

DORSET: Bridport Rd, Dorchester DT1 1RP (01305 250550)

DURHAM: County Hall, Durham DH1 5UL (0191 383 3253/3474)

ESSEX: County Hall, Victoria Rd South, Chelmsford CM1 1LX (01245 430067); Colchester & N.E. Essex Branch, Stanwell House, Stanwell St, Colchester CO2 7DL (01206 572099); Southend Branch, Central Library, Victoria Avenue, Southend on Sea SS2 6EX (01702 464278)

GLOUCESTERSHIRE: Clarence Row, Alvin St, Gloucester GL1 3DW (01452 425295)

HAMPSHIRE & THE ISLE OF WIGHT: Hampshire Record Office, Sussex St, Winchester SO23 8TH (01962 846154); Portsmouth City Records Office, Museum Rd, Portsmouth PO1 2LJ (01705 827261); Southampton City Records Office, Civic Centre, Southampton SO14 7LY (01703 832251); Isle of Wight Record Office, 26 Hillside, Newport, Isle of Wight PO30 2EB (01983 823820/1)

HEREFORD & WORCESTER: County Hall, Spetchley Rd, Worcester WR5 2NP (01905 766351); (Hereford Branch) The Old Barracks, Harold St, Hereford HR1 2QX (01432 265441); (Worcester Branch) St Helen's, Fish St, Worcester WR1 2HN (01905 765922)

HERTFORDSHIRE: County Hall, Hertford SG13 8DE (01992 555105)

HUMBERSIDE: County Hall, Champney Rd, Beverley HU17 9BA (01482 885007); Kingston upon Hull City Record Office, 79 Lowgate, Kingston upon Hull HU1 1HN (01482 595102); South Humberside Area Archive Office, Town Hall Square, Grimsby DN31 1HX (01472 353481)

KENT: Centre for Kentish Studies, County Hall, Maidstone ME14 1XQ (01622 694363); Canterbury City and Cathedral Archives, The Precincts, Canterbury CT1 2EH (01227 463510); Heritage Dept (SE Area), Folkestone Library, 2 Grace Hill, Folkestone CT20 1HD (01303 850123); Thanet Archive Office, Ramsgate Library, Guildford Lawn, Ramsgate CT11 9AI (01843 593532); Medway Area Archives Office, Civic Centre, Strood, Rochester ME2 4AW (01634 732714); West Kent Branch Office, Sevenoaks Library (01732 452384)

LANCASHIRE, LIVERPOOL & GREATER MANCHESTER: Lancashire Record Office, Bow Lane, Preston PR1 2RE (01772 263039); Greater Manchester Record Office, 56 Marshall St, New Cross, Manchester M4 5FU (0161 832 5284); Liverpool City Library (Record Office & Local History Dept), William Brown St, Liverpool L3 8EW (0151 225 5417); Merseyside Record Office, Cunard Building, Pier Head, Liverpool L3 1EG (0151 236 8038); Salford Archives Centre, 658/662 Liverpool Rd, Irlam, Manchester M44 5AD (0161 775 5643); Stockport Archive Service, Central Library, Wellington Rd South, Stockport SK1 3RS (0161 474 4530); Wigan Record Office, Town Hall, Leigh, Lancs WN7 2DY (01942 672421)

LEICESTERSHIRE & RUTLAND: Long St, Wigston Magna, Leicester LE18 2AH (0116 257 1080)

LINCOLNSHIRE: St Rumbolds St, Lincoln LN2 5AB (01522 526204)

LONDON: London Metropolitan Archives, 40 Northampton Rd, EC1R 0HB (0171 332 3820)

NORFOLK: Norfolk Record Office, Gildengate House, Anglia Square, Upper Green Lane, Norwich NR3 1AX (01603 761349)

NORTHUMBERLAND: Melton Park, North Gosforth, Newcastle upon Tyne NE3 5QX (0191 236 2680); Berwick upon Tweed Record Office, Borough Council House, Wallace Green, Berwick upon Tweed TD15 1ED (01289 330044); Morpeth Records Centre, The Kylins, Loansdean, Morpeth NE61 2EQ (01670 504084)

NOTTINGHAMSHIRE: County House, Castle Meadow Rd, Nottingham NG2 1AG (0115 958 1634)

NORTHAMPTONSHIRE: Wootton Hall Park, Northampton NN4 8BQ (01604 762129)

OXFORDSHIRE: County Hall, New Road, Oxford OX1 1ND (01865 815203)

SHROPSHIRE: Castle Gates, Shrewsbury SY1 2AQ (01743 255350)

SOMERSET: Obridge Rd, Taunton TA2 7PU (01823 337600)

STAFFORDSHIRE: County Buildings, Eastgate St, Stafford ST16 2LZ (01785 278373); Lichfield Joint Record Office, The Friary, Lichfield WS13 6QG (01543 256787)

SUFFOLK: (Ipswich) Gatacre Rd, Ipswich IP1 2LQ (01473 264541); (Bury St Edmunds) Raingate St, Bury St Edmunds IP33 2AR (01284 722522); (Lowestoft) Central Library, Clapham Rd, Lowestoft NR32 1DR (01502 503308)

SURREY: County Hall, Penryhn Rd, Kingston upon Thames KT1 2DN (0181 541 9065); Guildford Muniment Room, Castle Arch, Guildford GU1 3SX (01483 573942)

SUSSEX: East Sussex Record Office, The Maltings, Castle Precincts, Lewes, East Sussex BN7 1YT (01273 482349); West Sussex Record Office, Sherburne House, 3 Orchard St, Chichester PO19 1RN (01243 533911)

WARWICKSHIRE: Priory Park, Cape Rd, Warwick CV34 4JS (01926 412735)

WEST MIDLANDS: Birmingham Archives Division, Birmingham Central Library, Chamberlain Square, Birmingham B3 3HQ (0121 235 4217); Coventry City Records Office, Mandela House, Bayley Lane, Coventry CV1 5RG (01203 832418); Dudley Archives, Mount Pleasant St, Coseley, Dudley WV14 9JR (01902 880011); Wolverhampton Borough Archives, Central Reference Library, Snow Hill, Wolverhampton WV2 4AB (01902 717703)

WILTSHIRE: County Hall, Trowbridge BA14 8JG (01225 713139)

NORTH YORKSHIRE: North Yorkshire Record Office, Malpas Rd, Northallerton, North Yorkshire DL7 8AD (01609 777585); York City Archives Dept, Art Gallery Building, Exhibition Square, York YO1 2EW (01904 551879)

SOUTH YORKSHIRE: Barnsley Archive Service, Central Library, Shambles St, Barnsley S70 2JF (01226 773950); Doncaster Archives Dept, King Edward Rd, Balby, Doncaster DN4 0NA (01302 859811); Rotherham Archives Dept, Brian O'Malley Central Library and Arts Centre, Walker Place, Rotherham S65 1JH (01709 823616); Sheffield Archives, 52 Shoreham St, Sheffield S1 4SP (0114 273 4756)

WEST YORKSHIRE: Bradford District Archives, West Yorkshire Archive Service, 15 Canal Rd, Bradford BD1 4AT (01274 731931); Calderdale District Archives, Calderdale Central Library, Northgate House, Northgate, Halifax HX1 1UN (01422 392636); Kirklees District Archives, Kirklees Central Library, Princess Alexandra Walk, Huddersfield HD1 2SU (01484 442847); Leeds District Archives, Chapeltown Rd, Sheepscar, Leeds LS7 3AP (0113 262 8339)

WALES

CLWYD: The Old Rectory, Hawarden, Deeside CH5 3NR (01244 532364); (Ruthin) 46 Clwyd St, Ruthin LL15 1HP (01824 705180)

DYFED: Cardiganshire/Ceredigion Record Office, Swddfa'r Sir (County Hall), Aberystwyth, Dyfed SY23 3BU (01970 623816); Camarthenshire Record Office, County Hall, Camarthen, Dyfed SA31 1JP (01267 230837); Pembrokeshire Record Office, The Castle, Haverfordwest, Dyfed SA61 2EF (01437 763707)

GLAMORGAN: County Hall, Cathays Park, Cardiff CF1 3NE (01222 780282)

WEST GLAMORGAN: County Hall, Oystermouth Rd, Swansea SA1 3SN (01792 471589)

GWENT: County Hall, Cwmbran, Gwent NP44 2XH (01633 832214)

GWYNEDD: County Offices, Shirehall St, Caernarfon, Gwynedd LL55 1SH (01286 679088); Anglesey Area Record Office, Shirehall, Llangefni, Gwynedd LL77 7TW (01248 750262); Dolgellau Area Record Office, Cae Penarlag, Dolgellau, Gwynedd LL40 2YB (01341 422341)

POWYS: County Hall, Llandrindod Wells, Powys LD1 5LD (01597 826087/88)

Professional Researchers

For a list of reliable professional genealogists and record agents, send £1.50 (UK) or £1.85 or IRCs (overseas) to
The Association of Genealogists & Record Agents (AGRA)
Secretary, Mrs D Young
29 Badgers Close
Horsham
West Sussex RH12 5RU

For a list of reliable professional genealogists and record agents working personally in Scotland, send sae (UK) or 2 IRCs (overseas) to
Association of Scottish Genealogists & Record Agents (ASGRA)
P.O. Box 174
Edinburgh EH3 5QZ

For a list of reliable professional genealogists and record agents in Ireland, send 2 IRCs to
Association of Professional Genealogists in Ireland
c/o Genealogical Office
2 Kildare Street
Dublin 2

Family History Societies

Specific enquiries should be addressed to the relevant Society, but if in difficulty contact the Administrator for the Federation of Family History Societies, Mrs P. Saul, c/o The Benson Room, Birmingham & Midland Institute, Margaret Street, Birmingham B3 3BS.

BEDFORDSHIRE: Bedfordshire FHS, PO Box 214, Bedford MK42 9RX

BERKSHIRE: Berkshire FHS, Mr R. Houseman, The Corner House, Shaw Road, Reading RG1 6JX

BIRMINGHAM: Birmingham & Midland SGH, Mr M. Brittain, 111 Kenilworth Court, Coventry CV3 6JD

BRISTOL: Bristol & Avon FHS, Mrs A.C. Taylor, 103 The Downs, Portishead, Bristol BS20 8BE

BUCKINGHAMSHIRE: Buckinghamshire FHS, Mrs A. Hillier, 10 Merrydown, High Wycombe, Bucks

CAMBRIDGESHIRE: Cambridgeshire FHS, Mrs B. Ward, 1 Ascham Lane, Whittlesford, Cambs CB2 4NT

CHANNEL ISLANDS: Channel Islands FHS, Mrs S. Payn, PO Box 507, St Helier, Jersey, C.I.; La Soc Guernesiaise (FH Section), The Secretary, PO Box 314, Candie, St Peter Port, Guernsey, C.I. GY1 3TG

CHESHIRE: FHS Cheshire, Mrs H. Massey, 101 Irby Rd, Heswall, Wirral, Merseyside L61 6UZ; North Cheshire FHS, Mrs R. Walters, Windyridge, Jackson's Lane, Hazel Grove, Stockport SK7 5JW; South Cheshire FHS, Mr P.T. Johnson, 47 Thorn Rd, Halton Lodge, Runcorn, Cheshire WA7 5HJ

CLEVELAND: Cleveland FHS, Mr. A Sampson, 1 Oxgang Close, Redcar, Cleveland TS10 4ND

CORNWALL: Cornwall FHS, c/o 5 Victoria Square, Truro, Cornwall TR1 2RS

CUMBRIA (CUMBERLAND): Cumbria FHS, Mrs. M. Russell, 32 Granada Road, Denton, Manchester M34 2IJ; Furness FHS, Miss J. Fairburn, 64 Cowlarns Rd, Barrow-in-Furness, Cumbria LA14 4HJ

DERBYSHIRE: Derbyshire FHS, Mr G. Wells, Bridge Chapel House, St Mary's Bridge, Sowter, Derby DE1 3AT; Chesterfield & District FHS, Mr J. Robinson, Overhulme Farm, Cutthorpe, Chesterfield

DEVON: Devon FHS, Mrs E.M. Wilmot, 8 King Henry's Road, Exeter EX2 6AL

DORSET: Dorset FHS, Miss R. Clipson, 7 Coppercourt Leaze, Poole Rd, Wimborne, Dorset BH21 1QX (*see also* Somerset)

DURHAM: (*see* Cleveland and Northumberland)

ESSEX: East of London FHS, Mrs J. Taylor, 42 Alwen Grove, South Ockendon, Essex RM15 5DW; Essex FHS, Mr P. Moore, The Old Granary, Justice Wood, Polstead, Suffolk CO6 5DH; Waltham Forest FHS, Mr J. Bowen, 1 Gelsthorpe Road, Romford, Essex RM5 2NB

GLOUCESTERSHIRE: Gloucestershire FHS, Mr J. Loosley, Stonehatch, Oakridge Lynch, Stroud, Glos GL6 7NR (*see also* Bristol)

HAMPSHIRE: Hampshire Genealogical Society, Mrs R. Rawcliffe, 44 Southway, Bridgemary, Gosport, Hants PO13 0XD; Isle of Wight FHS, Mrs H. Lloyd, Rose Cott, Burnt House Lane, Newport, Isle of Wight PO30 2PW

HEREFORDSHIRE: Herefordshire FHS, Mr B. Donaldson, Halfar, Coldwells, Holmer, Hereford HR1 1LH

HERTFORDSHIRE: Hertfordshire F & Pop Hist Society, c/o The Secretary, 6 The Crest, Ware, Hertfordshire SG12 0RR; Royston & District FHS, Mrs Joyce Hellier, 60 Heathfield, Royston, Herts SG8 5BN

HUNTINGDONSHIRE: Huntingdonshire FHS, Mrs B.J. Browne, Lowood, Somersham, Huntingdon, Cambs PE17 3DL

ISLE OF MAN: Isle of Man FHS, Mr E.W.Q. Cleator, 5 Selborne Drive, Douglas, Isle of Man

KENT: Folkestone & District FHS, Miss J.M. Killick, 41 Reachfields, Hythe, Kent CT21 6LS; Kent FHS, Mrs J. Horwood, Westgate House, Dickley Wood, Maidstone, Kent ME17 1BL; North West Kent FHS, Hon. Sec, 6 Windermere Rd, Barnhurst, Bexleyheath, Kent DA7 6PW; Tunbridge Wells FHS, Mrs Oxenbury, The Old Cottage, Langton Rd, Tunbridge Wells, Kent TN3 0BA; Woolwich & District FHS, Mrs E. Reynolds, 54 Parkhill Rd, Bexley, Kent DA5 1HY

LANCASHIRE: Lancashire FH & HS, Mrs R. Hirst, 17 Victoria St, Haslingden, Rossendale, Lancs BB4 5DL; Liverpool & SW Lancs FHS, Miss P. Winker, 8 Paltridge Way, Pensby, Merseyside L61 5YG; Manchester & Lancs FHS, Mrs F. de Courcy, c/o Clayton House, 59 Piccadilly, Manchester M1 2AQ; North Meols FHS, Mr G. Wright, 44 Sunny Road, Southport, Lancs PR9 7LX; Ormskirk & District FHS, Mrs R. Janes, 85 Wigan Road, Westhead, Lathom, Lancs L40 6HY; Lancaster FHG, Mrs M. Wilmshurst, 94 Croston Rd, Garstang, Lancs PR3 1HR; Wigan FHS, Mr J. Mason, 464 Warrington Rd, Goose Green, Wigan, Lancs WN3 6QF

LEICESTERSHIRE: Leicestershire FHS, Miss D. Merryweather, 11 Faldo Close, Rushy Mead, Leicester LE4 7TS

LINCOLNSHIRE: Isle of Axholme FHS, Mr P. Threadgold, 4 Cheyne Walk, Bawtry, Doncaster DN10 6RS; Lincolnshire FHS, Mrs E. Robson, 135 Baldertongate, Newark, Notts NG24 1RY

MIDDLESEX: Hillingdon FHS, Mrs G. May, 20 Moreland Drive, Gerrards Cross, Bucks SL9 8BB; London & North Middlesex FHS, Mrs S. Lumas, 7 Mount Pleasant Rd, New Malden, Surrey KT3 3JZ; West Middlesex FHS, Miss Y. Woodbridge, 92 Nelson Road, Whitton, Twickenham, Middx TW2 7AY; Westminster & Central Middlesex FHS, Mr K. Rookledge, 2 West Ave, Pinner, HA5 5BY

NORFOLK: Norfolk FHS, Mrs Woolsey, Oak Cottage, Bellaport, Market Drayton, Shropshire TF9 4AZ; Mid-Norfolk FHS, Mr. T. Garland, 35 Colleen Close, Toftwood, Dereham, Norfolk NR19 1NL

NORTHAMPTONSHIRE: Northamptonshire FHS, Mrs A. Pegg, 19 Ridgway Road, Kettering, Northants NN15 5AQ; Peterborough & District FHS, Mr G. Harbron, 7 Newby Close, Peterborough PE3 6PU

NORTHUMBERLAND: Northumberland & Durham FHS, Mr J. Ashburner, 10 Melrose Grove, Jarrow on Tyne NE32 4HP

NOTTINGHAMSHIRE: Mansfield & District FHS, Mrs Enid M. Barber, 2 Cranmer Grove, Mansfield, Notts NG19 7JR; Nottinghamshire FHS, Miss S.M. Leeds, 10 Lyme Park, West Bridgford, Nottingham NG2 7TR

OXFORDSHIRE: Oxfordshire FHS, Mrs J. Kennedy, 19 Mavor Close, Woodstock, Oxford OX20 1YL

RUTLAND: (*see* Leicestershire)

SHROPSHIRE: Shropshire FHS, Mrs D. Hills, Redhillside, Ludlow Rd, Church Stretton, Shropshire SY6 6AD

SOMERSET: Burnham On Sea & Highbridge FHS, Mrs M. Betty, 1 Greenwood Close, West Huntspill, Somerset TA9 3SF; Somerset & Dorset FHS, Mr R. Steed, 7 Burch's Close, Galmington, Taunton, Somerset TA1 4TR; Weston-Super-Mare FHS, Mrs P. Hase, 15 Stanhope Rd, Weston-Super-Mare, Somerset BS23 4LP; (*see also* Bristol)

STAFFORDSHIRE: (*see* Birmingham)

SUFFOLK: Felixstowe FHS, Mrs J. Campbell, 7 Victoria Rd, Felixstowe, Suffolk IP11 7PT; Suffolk FHS, Mrs M. Barfield, 123 Cedarcroft Rd, Ipswich, Suffolk IP1 6BP

SURREY: East Surrey FHS, Mrs R. Turner, 27 Burley Close, London SW16 4QQ; West Surrey FHS, Mrs S. McQuire, Deer Dell, Botany Hill, The Sands, Farnham, Surrey GU10 1LZ

SUSSEX: Eastbourne & District FHS, Mrs P. Webb, 22 Abbey Road, Eastbourne, East Sussex BN20 8TE; Hastings & Rother FHS, Mr and Mrs Dawson, 65 Vale Rd, St Leonards on Sea, East Sussex TN37 6HA; Sussex FHG, Mrs J. Goddard, 54 Shirley Drive, Hove, Sussex BN3 6UF

WARWICKSHIRE: (*see* Birmingham); Coventry FHS, Mr G. Barwick, 61 Drayton Crescent, Eastern Green, Coventry CV5 7EL

WESTMORLAND: (*see* Cumbria)

WILTSHIRE: Wiltshire FHS, Mrs J. Rouse, 18 Sarsen Close, Okus, Swindon, Wilts SN1 4LA

WORCESTERSHIRE: (*see* Birmingham)

YORKSHIRE: Yorks Arch Society (F&PS Section) Mr J. Rayner, c/o YAS, Claremont, 23 Clarendon Road, Leeds LS2 9NZ

(EAST RIDING): City of York & District FHS, Ms J. Wilson, 4 Chestnut Ave, Stockton Lane, York YO3 0BR; East Yorkshire FHS, Mrs M.S. Oliver, 12 Carlton Drive, Aldbrough, East Yorks HU11 4SF

(NORTH RIDING): (*see* Cleveland, Ripon, East Yorkshire and City of York)

(WEST RIDING): Barnsley FHS, Mrs K. Wright, 58A High Street, Royston, Barnsley, S. Yorks S71 4RN; Bradford FHS, Mrs M. Pinchin, 152 Baildon Rd, Baildon, Shipley, W. Yorks BD17 6PU; Calderdale FHS, Mrs I. Walker, 61 Gleanings Avenue, Norton's Tower, Halifax HX2 0NU; Doncaster & District FHS, Mr J. Staniforth, 125 The Grove, Wheatley Hills, Doncaster DN2 5SN; Huddersfield & District FHS, Mrs M. Bowers, 31 Kingshead Road, Mirfield, W. Yorks WF14 9SJ; Keighley & District FHS, Mrs S. Daynes, 2 The Hallows, Shann Park, Keighley, W. Yorks BD20 6HY; Morley & District FHS, Mrs A. Dodgson, 23 Denshaw Drive, Morley, Leeds LS27 8RS; Ripon, Harrogate & District FHG, Mrs W.A. Symington, 18 Aspin Drive, Knaresborough, N. Yorks HG5 8HA; Sheffield & District FHS, Mr R. Bullen, 18 Furniss Avenue, Sheffield S17 3QL; Wharfedale FHG, Mr S.R. Merridew, 206 Mosely Wood Gardens, Cookridge, Leeds LS16 7JE

WALES

ANGLESEY: Gwynedd FHS, Mrs J. Hinde, Cwm Arian, Penysarn Fawr, Penysarn, Anglesey LL69 9BX

BRECONSHIRE: Powys FHS, Mrs J. Brown, Cwm Kesty Farmhouse, Newchurch, Kington, Powys

CAERNARFONSHIRE: (*see* Anglesey)

CARDIGANSHIRE: Cardiganshire FHS, Mrs S. Martin, Trebrysg, Tregaron, Ceredigion SY25 6LH; Dyfed FHS, Mrs A. Owen, Delfan, High Street, Llandysul, Ceredigion SA44 4DG
CARMARTHENSHIRE: (*see* Dyfed, Cardiganshire)
DENBIGHSHIRE: Clwyd FHS, Mrs A. Anderson, 3 Heol Berwyn, Cefn Mawr, Wrexham LL14 3NB
FLINTSHIRE: (*see* Denbighshire)
GLAMORGAN: Glamorgan FHS, Mrs M. Bullows, The Orchard, Penmark, Barry, S. Glamorgan CF62 9BN
MERIONETHSHIRE: (*see* Anglesey)
MONMOUTHSHIRE: Gwent FHS, Mrs N. Thomas, 11 Rosser St, Wainfelin, Pontypool NP4 6EA
MONTGOMERYSHIRE: Montgomeryshire GS, Mr S.W. Jones, 1 Moreton Rd, South Croydon, Surrey CR2 7DN: (*see also under* Breconshire)
PEMBROKESHIRE: (*see* Dyfed, Cardiganshire)
RADNORSHIRE: (*see* Breconshire)

IRELAND
Irish Gen Research Society, c/o The Irish Club, 82 Eaton Square, London SW1W 9AJ
South Down Family History Research, Mr P. Magennis, Old Technical Building, Downshire Road, Banbridge, Co. Down
North of Ireland FHS, Mr R.C. Davison, c/o QUB School of Education, 69 University Street, Belfast BT7 1HL
Dun Laoghaire Gen Society, Mr Michael Merrigan, 14 Rochestown Park, Dun Laoghaire, Co. Dublin
Irish FHS, PO Box 36, Naas, Co. Kildare, Eire

GUILD OF ONE-NAME STUDIES
Guild of One-Name Studies, Mr J. Isard, 74 Thornton Place, Horley, Surrey RH6 8RN

OTHER SOCIETIES (GENERAL)
Anglo-French FHS, Mr P. Pontet, 31 Collingwood Walk, Andover, Hants SP10 1PU
Anglo-German FHS, Mrs J. Towey, 14 River Reach, Teddington, Middx TW11 9QL
British Association of Cemeteries of S. Asia, Mr T. Wilkinson, 76½ Chartfield Avenue, London SW15 6HQ

Catholic FHS, Mrs B. Murray, 2 Winscombe Crescent, Ealing, London W5 1AZ

Huguenot & Walloon Research Association, Mrs J. Tsushima, 'Malmaison', Church Street, Great Bedwyn, Wilts SN8 3PE

International Soc for British Genealogy and Family History, PO Box 3115, Salt Lake City, Utah 84110-3115

Irish Genealogical Society International, PO Box 16585, St Paul, Minnesota 55116-0585

Jewish Genealogical Society of Great Britain, Ms Doreen Berger, 10 Dovercourt Gardens, Stanmore, Middlesex HA57 5SH

Krans-Buckland Family Association, Mrs J. Buckland, PO Box 1025, North Highlands, California 95660

Local Population Studies Society, Col Sir David Cooke Bt, 78 Harlow Terrace, Harrogate HG2 8AW

The Open University (DA301), Ms J. Eustace, Open University, Walton Hall, Milton Keynes MK7 6AA

Quaker FHS, Mr C. Pitt Lewis, 5 Rad Valley Gardens, Shrewsbury SY3 8AW

Genealogical Society of Utah (UK), Mr Geoffrey D. Mawlam, 185 Penns Lane, Sutton Coldfield, W. Midlands B76 1JU

Rolls Royce FHS, Mr K. Ranson, 25 Gisburn Road, Barnoldswick, Colne, Lancs BB8 5HB

OVERSEAS SOCIETIES

AUSTRALIA: Australian Inst of Gen Studies, PO Box 339, Blackburn, Victoria 3130; Society of Australian Genealogists, Richmond Villa, 120 Kent Street, Observatory Hill, Sydney 2000; Western Australian Gen Soc, 6/48 May Street, Bayswater, Western Australia 6053; Heraldry & Gen Soc of Canberra, GPO Box 585, Canberra, ACT 2601; Blue Mountains FHS, PO Box 97, Springwood, NSW 2776; Cape Banks FHS, PO Box 67, Marouba, NSW 2035; Dubbo MacQuarie FHS, PO Box 868, Dubbo, NSW 2830; Illawarra FHG, Mrs K. Alexander, PO Box 1652, Wollongong, NSW 2500; Lithgow & District FHS, PO Box 516, Lithgow, NSW 2790; Nepean FHS, PO Box 81, Emu Plains, NSW 2750; Newcastle FHS, PO Box 189, Adamstown, NSW 2289; Orange FHS, PO Box 930, Orange, NSW 2800; Richmond-Tweed FHS, Ms S. Warmerdam, PO Box 817, Ballina, NSW 2478; Shoalhaven FHS, Mrs C. Moorley, PO Box 591, Nowra, NSW 2541; Cairns & District FHS, Mrs B. O'Hara, PO Box 5069, Cairns, Queensland 4870; Central Queensland Family History Association, PO Box 6000, Rockhampton Mail Centre, Queensland

4702; Genealogical Society of Queensland, PO Box 423, Woolloongabba, Queensland 4102; Gold Coast & Albert Gen Soc, PO Box 2763, Southport, Queensland 4215; Gold Coast FH Research Group, PO Box 1126, Southport, Queensland 4215; Ipswich Genealogical Society, Mrs C. Robinson, PO Box 323, Ipswich, Queensland 4305; Maryborough District FHS, PO Box 408, Maryborough, Queensland 4650; Queensland FHS, PO Box 171, Indooroopilly, Brisbane, Queensland 4068; South Australian Gen & Her Society, GPO Box 592, Adelaide 5001, South Australia; Genealogical Society of Victoria, 5th Floor, Curtin House, 252 Swanston St, Melbourne 3000, Victoria; Genealogical Society of Tasmania, PO Box 60, Prospect, Tasmania 7250

CANADA: Alberta Family Histories Society, PO Box 30270, Station B, Calgary, Alberta T2M 4P1; Alberta Genealogical Society, #116, 10440-108 Avenue, Edmonton, Alberta T5H 3Z9, Canada; Alberta Gen Soc (Edmonton Branch), PO Box 754, Edmonton, Alberta T5J 2L4; British Columbia Gen Soc, PO Box 88054, Lansdowne, Richmond, British Columbia V6X 3T6; Victoria Genealogical Society, PO Box 45031, Mayfair Postal Unit, Victoria, British Columbia V8Z 7G9; Kamloops FHS, Box 1162, Kamloops, British Columbia V2C 6H3; Newfoundland & Labrador Gen Soc, Colonial Building, Military Road, St John's, Newfoundland A1C 2C9; British Isles FHS of Greater Ottawa, Box 38026, Ottawa, ON, K2C 1N0; Ontario Genealogical Society, Suite 102, 40 Orchard View Boulevard, Toronto, Ontario M4R 1B9; Quebec FHS, PO Box 1026, Postal Station Pointe Claire, Pointe Claire, Quebec H9S 4H9; Saskatchewan Genealogical Society, 1870 Lorne Street, Regina, Saskatchewan S4P 3E1

HOLLAND: Central Bureau Voor Genealogie, PO Box 11755, 2502 At The Hague, Netherlands

NEW ZEALAND: New Zealand Society of Genealogists, PO Box 8795, Auckland 3; New Zealand FHS INC, Mrs J. Lord, PO Box 13301, Armagh, Christchurch; Gen Research Inst of New Zealand, PO Box 36-107, Moera, Lower Hutt

SLOVAKIA: Slovak GHS at Matica Slovenska, Mgr Milan Sismis, Matica Slovenska, Novomeskeho 32, 036 52 Martin, Slovakia

SOUTH AFRICA: Gen Soc of South Africa, Suite 143, Postnet X2600, Houghton 2041, South Africa; West Rand FHS, Mr M. Tapping, PO Box 760, Florida 1710, South Africa; Human Sciences Research Council, Private Bag X41, Pretoria 0001

USA: British Isles FHS-USA, 2531 Sawtelle Boulevard, No. 134, Los Angeles, CA 90064-3163; Santa Barbara County Gen Soc, PO Box 1303, Santa Barbara, CA 93116-1303; Genealogical Assn of Sacramento, PO Box 292145, Sacramento, CA 95829-2145; Florida Genealogical Society, PO Box 18624, Tampa, Florida 33679-8624; Jefferson County Gen Soc, Box 174, Oskaloosa, Kansas 66066; English Gen Soc of Minnesota, PO Box 16069, St Paul, Minnesota 55116; Genealogical Forum of Oregon, 1410 S.W. Morrison, No. 812, Portland, Oregon 97205-1921; Bucks County Genealogical Society, PO Box 1092, Doylestown, Pennsylvania 18901; Utah Genealogical Society, Corresponding Secretary, UGS, PO Box 1144, Salt Lake City, Utah 84110-1144

Family History Centres
(The Church of Jesus Christ of Latter Day Saints)

Telephone the relevant centre to find out their opening times etc (and this may mean trying on several occasions as times differ), do not write, as staffing is limited to volunteers and they cannot respond to mail enquiries.

Aberdeen North Anderson Dr. AB2 6DD (01224 692206)
Belfast 401 Holywood Rd BT4 2GU (01232 768250)
Billingham Cleveland, The Linkway TS23 3HJ (01642 563162)
Bristol 721 Wells Rd BS14 9HU (01272 83836)
Cambridge 670 Cherry Hinton Rd CB1 4DR (01223 247010)
Cardiff Heol y Deri, Rhibwina, S. Glam CF4 6UH (01222 620205)
Carlisle Langrigg Rd, Morton Park (01228 26767)
Cheltenham Thirlestaine Rd G153 7AA (01242 523433)
Chester 30 Cliftone Drive, Blacon CH1 5LT (01244 390796)
Chorley 33-41 Walter St, Chorley (012572 69332)
Coleford Glos: Wynois Hill, Queensway (01594 832904)
Coventry Riverside Close, Whitley (01203 301420)
Crawley Sussex, Old Horsham Rd RH11 8PD (01293 516151)
Douglas IOM Woodside, Woodburn Rd (01624 75834)
Dublin The Willows, Finglas, Dublin 11 (01001 212265)
Dundee Bingham Terrace DD4 7HH (01382 451247)
Edinburgh 30a Colinton Rd E10 (0131 337 3049)
Exeter Wonford Rd, off Barrack Rd (01392 52703)
Glasgow 35 Julian Ave G12 0RB (0141 357 1024)

Grimsby Grimsby Ward Chapel, Linwood Ave, Waltham Rd (01472 828876)
Helston Clodgey Lane (01326 564503)
Hornchurch Essex, 64 Butts Green Rd (01424 58412)
Huddersfield 2 Halifax St, Birchencliffe (01484 420352)
Hull Springfield Way, Anlaby Common HU4 7RT (01482 572623)
Hull 725 Holderness Rd (01482 794250)
Ipswich 42 Sidegate Lane West IP4 3DB (01473 723182)
Jersey Rue de la Vallee, St Mary, St Helier (01534 82171)
Kilmarnock Whatriggs Rd (01563 26560)
Kings Lynn Reffley Lane (01553 67000)
Kirkaldy Winifred Cres. Forth Pk (01592 640041)
Lancaster Ovangle Rd (01524 33571)
Leeds Vesper Rd LS5 (01532 585297)
Lerwick Shetland (01595 5732)
Lichfield Purcell Ave WS17 7P (01543 414843)
Liverpool 4 Mill Bank Rd L13 0BW (0151 228 0433)
London 64/68 Exhibition Rd, S. Kensington SW7 2PA (0171 589 8561)
London 149 Nightingale Lane, Balham SW12 (0181 673 6741)
Londonderry Racecourse Rd, Belmont Estate (no telephone number)
Loughborough Thorpe Hill, Alan Moss Rd (01509 214991)
Luton corner London Rd/Cutenhoe Rd (01582 482234)
Maidstone 76b London Rd ME16 0DR (01622 757811)
Manchester Altrincham Rd, Wythenshawe M22 4BJ (0161 902 9279)
Mansfield Southridge Drive NG18 4FT (01623 26729)
Merthyr Tydfil Nantygwenith Rd, Georgetown (01685 722455)
Newcastle under Lyme Staffs; PO Box 285, The Brampton (01782 620653)
Newport IOW Chestnut Close, Shide Rd (01983 529643)
Northampton 137 Harlestone Rd NN5 (01604 51348)
Norwich 19 Greenways, Eaton NR4 7AX (01603 52440)
Nottingham Hempshill Lane, Bulwell NG6 8PA (01602 274194)
Paisley Campbell St, Johnstone PA5 8LD (01505 20886)
Peterborough Cottesmore Close, Netherton Estate (01733 263374)
Plymouth Hartley Chapel, Mannamead Rd PL3 (01752 668666)
Poole 8 Mount Rd, Parkstone BH14 0QW (01202 730646)
Portsmouth Kingston Crescent (01705 969243)
Rawtenstall Haslington Rd (01706 213460)
Reading 280 The Meadway, Tilehurst (0118 9410211)
Redditch 321 Evesham Rd, Crabbs Cross (01527 550657)
Rhyl Rhuddlan Rd (01745 331172)

Rochdale Tweedale St OL11 3TZ (01706 526292)
Sheffield Wheel Lane, Grenoside S30 3RL (01742 453231)
Staines 41 Kingston Rd TW14 0ND (01784 453823)
Sunderland Linden Rd, Queen Alexandra Rd (01915 285787)
Sutton Coldfield 185 Penns Lane (0121 384 2028)
Swansea Cockett Rd, Swansea (01792 585792)
Wednesfield Linthouse Lane (01902 724097)
Worthing Goring Street (01903 241829)
Yate Avon: Wellington Rd (01454 323004)
Yeovil Forest Hill (01935 26817)
York West Bank, Acomb (01904 798185)
(List kindly supplied by the LDS Family Service Centre, Birmingham)

Other Useful Addresses

SOCIETY OF GENEALOGISTS, 14 Charterhouse Buildings, Goswell Rd, London EC1M 7BA (0171 251 8799)
INSTITUTE OF HERALDIC & GENEALOGICAL STUDIES, Northgate, Canterbury, Kent CT1 1BA (01227 78664)
PUBLIC RECORD OFFICE, Ruskin Avenue, Kew, Richmond, Surrey TW9 4DU (0181 876 3444)
BRITISH LIBRARY NEWSPAPER LIBRARY, Colindale Avenue, London NW6 5HE (0171 323 7353)
FAMILY RECORDS CENTRE, 1 Myddelton Street, London EC1R 1UW (0181 392 5300)
THE PRINCIPAL REGISTRY OF THE FAMILY DIVISION, Somerset House, Strand WC2R 1LP (0171 936 7000)
FAMILY TREE MAGAZINE, 15/16 Highlode, Stocking Fen Rd, Ramsey, Huntingdon, Cambs PE17 1RB (01487 814051)
GENEALOGICAL RESEARCH DIRECTORY, 2 Stella Grove, Tollerton, Notts NG12 4EY
MAPS: DAVID & CHARLES, Brunel House, Newton Abbot, Devon; ALAN GODFREY, 57-58 Spoor Street, Dunston, Gateshead NE11 9BD

INDEX